Valor at Polebrook
The Last Flight of Ten Horsepower

8th U.S. Army Air Force

351st Bomb Group Insignia

510th Bomb Squadron Insignia

351st Bomb Group Aircraft Recognition Marking

Emblems and Markings Relevant to this Story

12/9/1998

I hope you enjoy our book!
I thank God for only by
his grace is it a reality!

Sincerely,

Rick Wood

Valor at Polebrook
The Last Flight of Ten Horsepower

Researched by Rick School
Written by Jeff Rogers

Valor at Polebrook

The Last Flight of Ten Horsepower

Copyright ©1998 by Rick School and Jeff Rogers
All rights reserved.
No part of this book may be reproduced
or copied without permission in writing
from the authors.

ISBN No. 0-9652491-5-8

Library of Congress No. 98-71188

Ken Cook Co.
9929 West Silver Spring Dr.
P.O. Box 25267
Milwaukee, WI 53225

Table of Contents

Acknowledgement vi

Dedication vii

Introduction................................. viii

Chapters

   1 Ten Men 1

   2 England 21

   3 Mission 81 33

   4 Back to England 49

   5 Landing 63

   6 On the Ground 75

   7 Post Mission, Post War 85

   8 Letters 105

Postscript 131

Bibliography 134

 # Acknowledgement

This book is the result of more than ten years of research and travel, and countless hours at the computer. During this time, we have had the pleasure of meeting many friendly, caring people who invited us into their homes and shared their memories with us. Without the kindness and sincerity of these wonderful folks, we could not have told this story. We'd like you to know who they are:

Howard and Wilmajean Stickford of the 351st Bomb Group Association, who got us started on the right track toward locating the people we needed to find; Joe and Margaret Rex; Joe Rex Jr.; Russell and Elsie Robinson; Tom and Margie Sowell; Elzia and Hazel Ledoux; The family of Ronald Bartley: Bonnie and Ed Brands, Juanita Linkswiler, Mary Stadick, and Bernice Boehm; Mrs. Ellen Moore; David Mathies; Joe Martin; Diane Pavlik (Lt. Nelson's niece); Ann Truemper Prestero; Ed Prestero; May Lane (Westmoreland) Owens; Dr. Frank Westmoreland; Members of the 351st Bomb Group Association: Elmer and Mary Ruschman, Ted Woodhave Jr., Peck and June Wilcox, Harold and Jean Flint, Michael Balkovich, Russell Ellersick, Joe Garcia, Lee Gingery, Donald Keith, Lundy Lunsford, Ferris Martin, Whitney Miller, Jack Seagraves, Norm Severson, Clay Snedegar, Joe Wroblewski, and all of the other 351st members who eagerly answered our questions; Harold Elder and Robert Roth (who flew with Ronald Bartley in Africa); William Lawley MOH, and his wife Amy; Witnesses and contributors in England: Sgt. Bill McElligott (Mathies NCO Academy, UK), David Clark, Mike Colton, Andrew Dick, Mrs. Farrington, Reginald Griffin, Arthur Pettifor, David Tower, and Mrs. Jean Whitaker; Contributors in the U.S.: MSgt. William Bennett USAF, Sgt. Vicki Schirkey USAF, authors Joe Bowman and the late Jeff Ethell; Our friends with the Experimental Aircraft Association in Oshkosh, Wisconsin: Daryl Lenz, Peter Moll, Jerry Walbrun, Verne Jobst, and Col. Harold Weekley USAF (ret.), who still flies B-17s more than fifty years after the war.

Special thanks goes to Eric Senf, who shared with us his knowledge of publishing; Mike Lombardi at Boeing Historic Archives, for interior photos of the B-17; Ann Moyers at the Medal of Honor Museum in Chattanooga, for Medal of Honor information and photos; Jay Foster, for proofreading our manuscript; and the Staff at Ken Cook Company, for their assistance in producing this book.

A very special thank you goes to our families and friends for their encouragement and their tactfully worded comments as the work progressed.

We would also like to express our sincere appreciation to Jim and Millie Barker, Bill and Murelle Dean, Whitney and Ruth Miller, Elmer and Mary Ruschman, and Walt and Dee Whitaker, without who's generous financial support this book could not have been published.

Rick School and Jeff Rogers

 # Dedication

This book is dedicated to the men of the 351st Bomb Group, and to the crew of Ten Horsepower. In memory of all who have fought for our freedom, and of those who gave their lives, let us never forget that our freedom has come at a very high price.

October 30, 1943 - The Crew of Ten Horsepower, in front of a B-17 at Alexandria, Louisiana. Kneeling, L - R: Lt. C. Richard Nelson, Flight Officer Ronald Bartley, Lt. Walter Truemper, Lt. Joe Martin. Standing, L - R: Sgt. Archie Mathies, Sgt. Joe Rex, Sgt. Carl Moore, Sgt. Russell Robinson, Sgt. Thomas Sowell, Sgt. Magnus "Mac" Hagbo.

Introduction

In 1978, as a student in the eighth grade, Rick School read a book entitled *The Big Week* by Glen Infield. Infield's book recalls the U.S. Army Air Force bomber strikes against German aircraft factories from February 20 to 25, 1944. Many missions were detailed in the book, but Rick was most enthralled by a story which described the action aboard a B-17 named Ten Horsepower. With their copilot dead and their pilot unconscious, members of the crew had to fly the plane back to England and try to make a landing. Rick didn't know that the account he was reading was not accurate, or that he would one day meet many of the people he was reading about.

In 1988 Rick began to search for more information about the bomber crew he had learned of ten years earlier. This book is the result of that effort, but writing a book was not Rick's first objective. Through his interest in military aviation, Rick had become a collector of aviation art prints. When he realized that no one had done a painting of Ten Horsepower, he decided to commission such a work. Artist David Poole was chosen to create the painting, but oil could not touch canvas until more of the story was learned. What model of B-17 was Ten Horsepower? What markings did it have? How badly damaged was the plane? Where did it crash? How many of the crew survived? Are any still alive? Where do they live now? When Rick chose to find the answers himself, he had no idea that his search would become an ongoing project that would span another ten years.

Ten Horsepower was an olive-drab-over-gray B-17G, serial number 42-31763. It is not clear whether the plane's name or artwork adorned its nose but it is undeniable that the ten men who flew in it on February 20th, 1944 became the most decorated bomber crew in Eighth Air Force history.

On only their second mission, these men were frustrated by a long delay before take-off. They felt a fearful anticipation while searching the sky for enemy fighters, then the adrenaline surge when those fighters attacked. They learned the shocking suddenness of cannon shells exploding inside the plane, and the sickening sight of death in the cockpit. They experienced the helplessness of being pinned to the floor by centrifugal force as their bomber spiraled toward the ground. Miraculously, the falling plane was brought under control. By then, neither pilot could fly. Some men bailed out. Others stayed with the ship. In the end, with the navigator in the radio room and the ball turret gunner in the copilot's seat, the plane crashed on a tree-topped hill four miles from its base.

These sketchy details only begin to relate the events of that day. For years afterward, the story of how crewmen Walter

Valor at Polebrook

Truemper and Archie Mathies earned posthumous Medals of Honor was told and retold. Over time, the literary zeal of numerous authors has done much to distort history. Some ignore the significant contributions made by scared or wounded crewmen at their stations aft of the cockpit. One popular book places some of the crewmen in two separate aircraft. Eventually, one of these inaccurate accounts led to Rick School's search for the facts, but only through hundreds of phone calls, continuous letter writing, and nationwide road travel did he learn how radically the story had been altered. This book is intended to set the record straight.

Rick has traveled extensively to research this story. He has personally met and interviewed three surviving crewmembers from Ten Horsepower, and has corresponded with a fourth. Much has been learned from the pilot of a B-17 sent aloft to assist the crippled bomber. Rick has attended several 351st Bomb Group reunions, one of which entailed a trip to Polebrook, England, the wartime home of the group. Many people who were involved in the February 20 mission provided firsthand, eyewitness accounts of the attack on Ten Horsepower, and of the efforts to bring it safely home.

The military account of the flight has been learned from Army Air Force mission reports and aircrew service records. Airmen's flight logs and personal diaries add a behind-the-scenes perspective to events leading up to the mission. Several aviation reference books provided descriptions of operations at Eighth Air Force bomber bases. Other details were found in newspapers and periodicals printed during the war.

Some of the most descriptive and personal information about the men of Ten Horsepower came from their surviving family members. All who could be located willingly shared their memories. Some donated photos and mementos, including letters written by the crewmen themselves. At times it was very awkward to ask questions, knowing that old wounds were being re-opened, and the pain of the families' losses recalled. Even so, all of the relatives Rick contacted wanted to preserve the memory of their loved ones. The authors extend to them a deep respect and appreciation for their contributions to our work.

The air war in Europe consumed an incredible number of aircraft. Stories of life or death struggles were commonplace, and damaged airplanes could be seen limping back to base on any given day. Thousands of young airmen were forced to bail out, or to continue flying and fighting after their planes were shot up and they themselves were wounded. In many ways this book tells their stories too, for all left families and friends behind, traveled from base to base during military training, and eventually crossed an ocean to go and fight for freedom. The courage and sacrifices of these people are not to be overlooked, but it must be left to other artists to portray their heroism. The focus of *Valor at Polebrook* is on what ten people thought, felt, and did as the crew of an airplane named Ten Horsepower. This is the story of how ordinary men placed in extraordinary circumstances became, if only for a few hours, extraordinary men. And, based on the words of those who were there, this is the way it really happened.

Jeff Rogers - January, 1998

THE PAINTING THAT STARTED IT ALL
(AND HOW YOU CAN OWN A COPY)

In August of 1991, after three years of waiting, I was finally able to display the painting of Ten Horsepower. Artist David Poole did an excellent job of portraying the desperate last moments of the aircraft and the men still on board. After hearing many positive comments from my friends and co-workers, it occurred to me that other people might also appreciate this dramatic painting. So, I made arrangements for production of 500 Limited Edition prints. These prints are now available for collection and display in your home, office, or personal art gallery.

Overall print size is 32-1/4 by 23-1/2 inches, with an image size of 27-1/2 by 17-3/4 inches. Each print is hand-signed by the artist, by three of the men who flew in Ten Horsepower on February 20, 1944, and by the pilot of the aircraft shown flying alongside during the efforts to land at Polebrook. The selling price is $125.00. (Wisconsin residents add 5% sales tax.) Please include an additional $10.00 shipping and handling.

To order your Limited Edition print of Valor at Polebrook, please send your check (payable to Rick School) to Rick School, P.O. Box 83, Kimberly, WI 54136. Call (920) 730-8212 for information on print availability and shipping dates. The phone number may change, but the P.O. Box will remain available for your orders.

This address may also be used to order additional copies of this book at the mail order price of $28.00. This includes sales tax and shipping. Thank you for your order.

 # Chapter One: Ten Men

In the second week of September, 1943, on a troop train out of Peyote, Texas, twenty-five year old Archibald Mathies searched through the crowded coaches while trying to match four faces to the names on the list in his hand. The young airman was a long way from home but, to Mathies, travel was nothing new.

Private Archie Mathies, U.S. Army. Archie signed this photo "To the sweetest of all, My Mother". (Photo courtesy of David Mathies)

"Archie" Mathies was born in Stonehouse, Lanarkshire, Scotland on June 3, 1918. His parents, William and Mary Mathies, immigrated to the United States three years later and settled in Finleyville, Pennsylvania. After graduating from high school, Archie went to work for the Pennsylvania Coal Company and joined his father at the Montour #10 mine in the town of Library. Archie enlisted in the Army on December 20th, 1940. After basic training, he entered Airplane Mechanic School at Chanute Field, Illinois. He graduated in October of 1941 and was posted first to a base in New York, and later to one in North Carolina. In February and March of 1943, now as a Sergeant, Archie attended Flexible Gunnery School at Tyndall Field, Florida. That July, he was sent to Peyote for operational training.

Through his education and experience, Sgt. Mathies had qualified as flight engineer. His flying duties would be to watch over his plane, a B-17 heavy bomber, and to keep track of any mechanical problems or repairs needed. Mathies would be a gunner, and would also be in charge of the other five Sergeants assigned to his crew. His first task was to locate some of these airmen on the train.

Twenty-three year old Sgt. Thomas R. Sowell was bored by the inactivity of the long train ride. He passed the time by talking, joking, and smoking with some of

Valor at Polebrook

the other fliers on board. Tall and lean, Sowell had been born in Arkansas but considered himself a Texan as he had lived in that state for most of his life. His Southern drawl and country dialect could give no other impression. Sowell's orders were identical to those carried by most of the other men on the train: Proceed to Alexandria, Louisiana for crew assignment and combat aircrew training.

Sowell had previously attended aircraft maintenance school at Shepperd Field in Wichita Falls, Texas. He also became a flight engineer, and received specialized training in the autopilot system of the B-17. Following gunnery school in Kingman, Arizona, Sowell returned to Texas for assignment to a B-17 squadron: "I was sent to Peyote, Texas, a big base out in the middle of a land the Devil himself wouldn't have. There were a lot of us, just extra gunners for the pool. We were supposed to get on a crew down there, and the one I got was a bunch of alcoholics. They went out the day before I was to start flying with them and bombed a Mexican's barn and killed a cow. That crew was busted up right then. Then they sent me by train to Alexandria, and on that train I met Archie Mathies. He was coming down the aisle, asking for Thomas R. Sowell. Archie and Carl had a list, and they were looking for me."

"Carl" was twenty-five year old Sgt. Carl W. Moore, of Williamsport, Pennsylvania. Like Mathies and Sowell, Sgt. Moore was a flight engineer and gunner. Carl Moore had a beautiful singing voice which he shared through his work with his church choir. Like others who heard Moore sing, Tom Sowell was greatly impressed: "Some GI on the train was drunk, and he was trying to sing 'God Bless America'. Carl walked over to him, real friendly, and said 'Here, let me show you how that one goes.' It was amazing how beautifully Carl could sing. He finished the song, then asked other people on board to join in, but no one would because of how well Carl sang."

Sgt. Russell Robinson. At the age of 27, Robinson was the oldest on the crew.

The next man on Archie's list was Sgt. Russell Robinson, from Springfield, Colorado. Robinson was a calm, matter-of-fact country man who left his tractor mechanic's job in September of 1942 to become a fighter pilot. Robinson completed his twenty-seventh birthday before completing his pilot qualification exams, for which the maximum age was twenty-six. He trained instead as an airplane armorer and gunner. As his new crewmates got to know him, they'd find Russell to be a level headed fellow, very low keyed, and friendly.

The last man on the list was also the youngest. Twenty-one year old Sgt. Joseph F. Rex, from Defiance, Ohio, had been through basic electronics and radio communication training before being posted to Peyote. He would be the ears and voice of his crew. Rex was a reserved young man with deep religious values. Joe Rex didn't drink or gamble, but he was regarded as a formidable opponent at the pinochle table.

Sergeants dressed for parade. Left to right - Archie Mathies, Joe Rex, Carl Moore.

Because of the war, the city of Alexandria had grown from its peacetime size of 40,000 inhabitants to become a temporary home for more than 200,000 U.S. Servicemen. Each week, hundreds of new pilots, navigators, bombardiers, and gunners arrived to complete the last phase of their training before deploying overseas. By September 15th the five Sergeants had settled into their new quarters. They soon met the other men assigned to their crew, among them Sgt. Magnus Hagbo from Seattle, Washington. "Mac" Hagbo had been through Flexible Gunnery School, but was not a mechanic. Hagbo and Tom Sowell became good friends, and of all on the crew, Sowell knew him best: "Mac was a good old Norwegian. He was real witty. I wouldn't want to describe his sense of humor on the radio, but he was very intelligent. Mac was the son of a longshoreman. They'd go out fishing, and they'd stay months out on the ocean. Mac said he read a lot out at sea. Sometimes he'd talk in words I couldn't understand, and I'd have to get out the dictionary.

"The army gave us a test to see how much we had learned from school, and Hagbo made almost a perfect score. Now, he only had a seventh or eighth grade education. They gave him another test, and he scored even higher still. And the army said, 'There isn't a man alive who can get this high a score without any schooling.' Well, they didn't know that Mac had gotten a job at a Washington State prison, working with the inmates in an education program. And Mac said 'I didn't give this test to the prisoners at Walla Walla all those years for nothing!' I guess that's why he was quiet much of the time. He was probably just thinking a lot."

There was a lot for Hagbo and the others to think about. They would be in Alexandria for just over two months. In that time they had to learn how to work with a B-17 squadron, and with each other. The inexperienced men would need first rate leadership to mold them into a crew that could hit the target and make it home alive. Their ultimate survival would depend on the ability of their pilot and crew commander. This would be Clarence Richard Nelson Jr., a twenty-four year old Lieutenant from Brookfield, Illinois. Known by family and friends as "Dick", Nelson had been born in Chicago on May 4th, 1919. When he was quite young, Nelson's family moved to Hollywood, California, but returned to Illinois while Dick was still of grade school age. Nelson grew up in

Valor at Polebrook

Riverside, near Brookfield. He was very outgoing and made friends easily. In high school, Nelson shared his personality through involvement in chorus and dramatics. After graduation in spring of 1937, he found employment at the Hawthorne Works of the Western Electric Company. The technical atmosphere of his new job appealed to Nelson so much that in fall of 1938 he entered the freshman class of the School of Engineering at Purdue University. Dick Nelson did well in his studies, but as he saw how the world was changing, other matters became important to him. He had not yet completed his second year of college when he decided to join the Army.

Clarence Richard Nelson, Jr.

Nelson's enlistment in the Army gave no hint that he would become an accomplished pilot and crew leader for whom his men would risk their lives. During the war, in a journal entitled *A Resume of Our Pilot's Life in the Service of His Country*, Mrs. Florence Nelson wrote about her son's time with the U.S. military. Excerpts from the journal follow Nelson's path to Alexandria:

"*Clarence Richard Nelson Jr. left Riverside, Illinois on April 21st, 1941. He was sent to Camp Grant in Rockford, Illinois, where he remained for two days. He then went by train to Camp Forrest, Tullahoma, Tennessee. He of course entered the army as a 'rookie', and as green as they come regarding GI affairs. However, he entered into the spirit of camp life and resolved to get all he could out of the training. To ease matters a little, Dad and I drove down to see him over Memorial Day, and took him and six of his buddies on a sightseeing trip through Tennessee, which is noted for its relics of the Civil War. We were with the boys for three days and there was much sadness at our parting. We promised them more such treats in the future if they behaved themselves!*

"*On August 2nd, Dick left C.F. for the first of his maneuvers, which are Army training away from camp. The boys get to see the country, as these maneuvers extend into several states. After returning, Dick was placed in a medical battalion with a pal whom he has affectionately dubbed 'Doc'. Dick worked faithfully at his training, and was rewarded* with his furlough. He and several of his buddies came home on October 28th and remained here until November 15th. Before his furlough, he was promoted to PFC and we rejoiced with him at this news. The boys wrote us there would be no furlough for the holidays and begged us to drive down again. It was arranged, and we invited Doc's mother to accompany us. We were with our boys for Christmas, having dinner with them in the mess hall, and had a jolly time. While with Dick, he confided in us that he was neither happy nor satisfied in the Medics and had therefore applied for a transfer to the Army Air Corps. He told us this course was a mighty stiff one and he would be in school most of the time while in training. He made application and awaited results. In February of 1942, we learned the application had been accepted.

"Dick left Camp Forrest and all his buddies in June of 1942, and traveled to Craig Field, Selma, Alabama, where he received his first phase of Air Corps training. Dick left Craig on September 1st, '42 for Nashville, Tennessee where he received his classification. Originally, his desire was to be a bombardier, for which he trained at Craig. Upon arrival at Nashville, he applied for pilot's training. He was given tests that he passed, then was sent to his next field.

"Dick's first steps for pilot training at Maxwell Field, Montgomery, Alabama, were completed in a short time. He left Maxwell on December 1st for Tuscaloosa, Alabama, where he was given the rank of A/C Lieutenant in the 51st AAF Flying Training Detachment as A/C Group Supply Officer. Dick went to Newport AAFTC, at Newport, Arkansas, sometime in February of '43. On March 3rd, he was raised to the rank of Corporal in the AAF Basic Flying School. His training here was brief, as he left on or about March 25th.

"Dick arrived at Blytheville, Arkansas on March 26th, 1943 to begin the last lap of his pilot training. While at Blytheville, he wrote home he was flying a B-25, the same type of plane major Jimmy Doolittle flew when he bombed Tokyo. He also wrote he had flown the B-17, for which he showed a decided preference, having remarked, 'The Fort is my baby.' At Blytheville, he also specialized in high altitude flying. On May 28th, Dick was graduated from the advanced flying school, and received the much coveted 'WINGS'. These exercises were very serious, solemn, and dignified. They were extremely impressive, and the cadets seemed to realize they were approaching the threshold of responsibility. Dad, Dorothy, Virginia, and I were on hand to congratulate Lieutenant Nelson, officer in the United States Army Air Force, as he came from the platform carrying his well-earned 'WINGS'. He came immediately to us and pinned HIS WINGS on 'My Mom, my best girl'. At this time, we had the pleasure of meeting 'the young lady', Miss May Lane Westmoreland of Memphis, Tennessee, whom Dick had invited to be his guest for the graduation festivities. After the

Valor at Polebrook

exercises, we all had dinner at the hotel, then Dick and May Lane left us to change to evening attire for the big military Ball to be given in the evening. Dick was even more handsome in his new officers' summer uniform, and May Lane looked like a breath of spring in her new ruffled red and white organdie, an orchid nestled in her curls, as they came down to meet us in the hotel gardens. Under Dick's arm he carried two florists boxes containing corsages for his Mom and 'Big' sister. This little act of thoughtfulness was another proof of Dick's affection for his loved ones.

C. Richard Nelson, Sr., and his wife, Florence, congratulate their son Dick upon his graduation from advanced flight training, Blytheville, Arkansas, May 28, 1943. The "wings" Nelson presented to his mother are faintly visible in the photo.

"After the excitement of graduation was over, the members of the class were given a four day vacation. Dick left Blytheville on May 31st for Sebring, Florida. We drove back home after a delightful time with 'OUR PILOT.' Dick arrived at Hendricks Field, in Sebring on June 2nd, at the Student Officer's Section, and to study more thoroughly the big bombers in which he had decided to specialize. He transferred to Peyote, Texas on July 14th to begin his first phase training in advanced flying on the Fortress. In September, Dick received a much earned, week-long furlough. Dad and I met him at the airport on September 6th. It was a very happy homecoming. Stratton and Althea [Nelson's brother and sister-in-law] came home from New Jersey to be here at the reunion, and May Lane came up from Memphis. All the family was here but Bob, who had to remain in Camp in Frederick, Maryland. It was all too short, but was glorious while it lasted. Dick and May Lane flew back to Memphis on September 12th. He then reported to Alexandria, Louisiana to begin final phase training."

The Flying Fortress was a big, slow airplane, stable in flight, but heavy on the controls. Lt. Nelson was still a relatively low-time pilot, and the men kidded him that some of his landings were not as smooth as they would have liked them to be. Even so, Nelson flew his bomber with a capable hand and sound judgment. He knew that when he was in the left seat, nine other men counted on him for their safety. Lt. Nelson did not take that responsibility lightly. He intended to use the practice flights out of Alexandria to give basic flight instruction to some of the crewmembers. Nelson knew that he could be killed or wounded in battle. If the worst happened, untrained men could not fly the complex airplane for any great distance, but perhaps one of the crew could hold the plane steady while the others bailed out. In any event, by teaching his men some simple fundamentals of flying, Nelson would be increasing their chances of survival.

Flight Officer Ronald Bartley

Flight Officer Ronald E. Bartley of Underwood, North Dakota would sit across from Lt. Nelson in the cockpit. The twenty-two year old copilot was no stranger to airplanes, but his military service had not started in the Army Air Force. Ronald Bartley had applied for flight training immediately after his first airplane ride. That had been in November of 1941 while he was still a buck private in the Army at McChord Field in Washington State. Ronald wrote about the flight in a letter to his sister, Mary: *"I talked one of the pilots into taking me for a ride in the pilot trainer ship the other day. Boy, was that fun! He did every stunt he new trying to make me sick, but no luck. Then he let me fly it for a while. I sure think I'm going to like pilot training, if I ever get to go to school. Hope I get to go pretty soon..."*

But the chance to fly didn't come as quickly as Bartley wanted it to. In a letter dated February 5th, 1942, Ronald told his family, *"I applied for Officer's Training yesterday. Maybe I'll be lucky enough to get into that, (I hope). I might still get into pilot training, too. I'll try for anything that comes along now, you know. There is nothing lower or worse than being a buck private."*

The discouraged soldier managed to transfer into the Army Air Force as an electronics student, and found himself training as a radio operator/gunner. Bartley was challenged by the technical nature of radio communications. He spent many nights in the barracks with his notes and books spread across his bunk. His studies left little time for socializing.

Bartley changed bases several times during his electronics training. His parents and sisters followed him around the country by reading the postmarks on the letters he sent home. Whether handwritten or typed, Ronald's notes were punctuated with his sense of humor and his fondness for his family. He was lonely, moving from base to base, and he longed for news of the daily lives of his loved ones. On the average, Ronald wrote three or four times a month.

Valor at Polebrook

On duty in the desert. From left to right, Radio Operator Ronald Bartley, Crew Chief W. A. Stephenson, Copilot R. M. Wright, Gunner L. Diehl, Pilot H. T. Elder, and Bombardier / Navigator C. Murdoch. Sad Music was a B-25 assigned to the 434th Squadron, 12th Bomb Group (M), North Africa, 1942.

Bartley's writing habits changed in July of 1942 when the 434th squadron of the 12th Bomb Group (M) was sent into battle. As a radio operator and gunner on B-25s, Sgt. Bartley helped push Rommel's Afrika Korps and elements of the Italian Army out of Egypt during late 1942 and early 1943. For nine months, Ronald was flying combat in the Middle East. A few letters did reach his family but censorship prevented him from telling them exactly where he was or what he was doing.

Bartley rotated home in April of 1943. He could have continued his service as a radio operator, but he still wanted to fly. Soon after his return to the States, Ronald surprised everyone by getting married. Then, after a brief honeymoon, he and his new bride, the former Bernice Adams, traveled to San Antonio, Texas, where Bartley entered flight training. The new pilot progressed quickly. When he wasn't flying a plane, he was logging time in a classroom with other student pilots. In June he wrote home complaining of a spell of bad weather and how it had added to his already busy flying schedule. He took it in stride though. That letter ended with, *"Oh,*

Ten Men

Student Pilot Ronald Bartley (at right) and two unidentified airmen stand near a T-6 Texan training aircraft. Few pilots of this era completed flight training without logging time in a T-6.

well. It's all in a lifetime." Ronald Bartley's lifetime would be immeasurably shortened by his decision to become a pilot.

Bartley graduated from flight school at Lubbock Army Air Field, Texas, on August 30th, 1943. He was promoted to the rank of Flight Officer, not having had the formal officer's training that would have earned him his Lieutenant's bars. After a brief furlough, Ronald and his wife packed their few possessions and headed for Louisiana.

Flight Officer Bartley's time in Alexandria would be vital to the development of his flying skills. Although he was a good pilot, he didn't have the feel for landing the larger, heavier bomber types. Sitting in the copilot's seat, Bartley would continue his training under the guidance of Lt. Nelson.

Flying the massive Fortress would require all of the pilots' attention and would leave them little time to keep track of where they were. This job fell on the shoulders of Lt. Walter E. Truemper, the twenty-four year old navigator from Aurora, Illinois.

Truemper's military career began in June of 1942 when he was inducted into the Army. His first assignment was to an artillery battery, but in November of 1942 he was appointed Aviation Cadet and sent to San Antonio, Texas to begin preliminary flight training. Truemper began navigation school in January of 1943 at Ellington Field, Texas. He made excellent progress and completed basic navigation in March. Cadet Truemper spent two months in gunnery school, then moved on to advanced navigation training at Hondo Army Air Field, Texas. He completed this course on August 26th and was commissioned a Second Lieutenant with the rating of Navigator. Lt. Truemper possessed an uncommon navigational ability which was immediately recognized by his superiors. The young officer was slated for a training job in the States, but Walter didn't want to

Walter Truemper upon graduation from Navigator training in August of 1943.

Valor at Polebrook

be an instructor. He wanted to contribute directly to the effort to end the war, and asked to be assigned to an operational squadron. In early September he joined the 796th Bombardment Squadron at Alexandria, Louisiana.

Joe Martin (left) and Walter Truemper suited up for a training flight out of Alexandria. Oct. 27, 1943.

The last man to join the crew was the bombardier, twenty-four year old Lt. Joseph R. Martin, from Burlington, New Jersey. Like the other officers on the crew, Joe Martin's service life did not begin anywhere close to an airfield. Martin entered the Army in January of 1941, and became a Section Leader in an infantry unit. In March of 1942 Corporal Martin became Cadet Martin and was transferred to Kelly Field, Texas, for preliminary flight training. By July, Martin had accumulated 100 hours of flight time but had been eliminated from further pilot training for an unspecified flying deficiency. Martin next entered navigator school in Hondo, then transferred to bombardier training in Midland, Texas, completing that course in March of 1943. He returned to navigator training, but again did not finish. After gunnery school in Kingman, Arizona, Martin reported for operational training at Peyote, Texas, in early September, 1943. During the following two weeks, he logged 40 hours in the nose of a B-17. Martin was an excellent bombardier. On the training flights he demonstrated a consistent accuracy which distinguished him from others in his group. Lt. Joe Martin arrived in Alexandria on September 23, 1943.

Before being assigned to Alexandria, the men had trained as individuals to learn their specialties. Now each man had to learn to work with nine others as part of a team. Every aspect of operating their bomber had to be learned, and most of them were practiced in the air. The flights were planned to simulate the long distance missions the crew would be flying once they went overseas. More than once, Russell Robinson felt that the ground below looked familiar: "We flew back over Texas a lot, sometimes around Peyote. There were a lot of oil wells down around there. At night, we could see the burn offs from the oil fields, the natural gas they burn from the wells. We had gunnery practice from the plane during the day. We shot at targets on the ground from low altitude. That was kind of interesting. We were flying around in the heat of the day at low altitude over Texas. The air currents rising up from the desert made for some rough flying."

While the gunners were clinging to their guns, sometimes more for support against the turbulence than for aiming, Nelson, Bartley, and Truemper were combining their talents to get their plane to the target range and back. Navigator Truemper had three methods of determining their position and desired course. These were pilotage, radio, and celestial navigation. Nelson and Bartley were already familiar with pilotage. This was simply a matter of keeping track of where the plane was by visually sighting landmarks and known points of reference. Pilotage depended on the pilots' familiarity with the area, and was of little use at night or when cloud cover obscured the ground.

For radio navigation Lt. Truemper could choose a radio station on the ground and tune his radio compass to pick up its signal. By turning a loop-shaped antenna on the plane's belly, Truemper could determine the compass bearing to that station. This system was called the radio direction finder, or RDF. The direction was displayed on an indicator at the navigator's table, and on an identical gauge on the pilot's instrument panel. Either Nelson or Truemper could tune the receiver for directional information.

Another application of radio navigation required the help of Sgt. Rex. Using Morse code, Rex would transmit the letters "QDM". This was a request for the ground station to determine the position of the aircraft. With contact established, Rex would hold his transmitter key for thirty seconds while the ground station homed in on his signal. The ground operator would then report the magnetic bearing from the plane to that station. Both of these systems provided the pilots with a way to determine direction if the navigator was out of action.

Celestial navigation was more complex than RDF or pilotage, and depended entirely on the skill of the navigator. For centuries it has been known that at given times specific stars will be visible at positions above the horizon, and that they will form measurable and calculable angles and lines in relation to the horizon. By "shooting" the stars with a sextant, Lt. Truemper could measure the angles and "draw" the lines which would in theory intersect at one point, i.e., the location of the bomber. Due to the movement of the aircraft between sightings, it was considered accurate if the position was isolated to within a five mile triangle.

Celestial navigation was only useable at night. It required a strong knowledge of the stars, and keen mathematical ability. The gambling Sgt. Sowell soon learned that Walter Truemper possessed both of these tools: "We'd leave out of Alexandria, say, going to El Paso, and I'd say, 'Trump, give me three minutes?', and he'd say, 'Yeah'. And I'd bet him that he'd miss the checkpoint in El Paso or wherever by more than three minutes, and I'd give him odds. I never did win anything. Truemper was too good a navigator."

Lt. Joe Martin was gaining valuable experience. The practice flights sometimes involved simulated bomb runs against towns or villages, with prominent buildings designated as "targets". Martin only dropped bombs on the live firing ranges. Sowell recalls the confidence the crew had in their bombardier's ability: "Joe Martin was the best professional on the team. He dropped those bombs right on the bulls eye, every time. We'd get the pictures back, and when everybody else was hitting around the 300 yard mark, old Joe was hitting right in the center. He was an excellent bombardier."

Copilot Bartley was steadily learning the fine points of handling the B-17, but he was still having difficulty landing the massive plane. It was a problem that bothered Sergeant Sowell: "Flight Officer Bartley could really fly that formation. He

Valor at Polebrook

could put the wingtip close to the waist of the plane next to us and still keep it out of the propwash. But he couldn't land a kite on a windy day. He'd make one approach and five landings... bounce, bounce, bounce, bounce..."

On one flight it seemed to Sgt. Sowell that the copilot's feel had improved remarkably. The lanky Texan later learned that Joe Martin had been flying during what were supposed to be Bartley's landings. Russell Robinson recalls that Lt. Martin wasn't the only other crewman to fly the plane from the copilot's seat: "Lt. Nelson let everybody up front to fly the plane. He'd tell us what to do. He showed us how to coordinate rudder and ailerons to make the right kind of turns. If you pushed the control column forward, the plane went down. If you pulled it back, the plane went up. It seemed heavy on the controls. You had to pull back pretty hard to make it go up. And you had to use quite a bit of aileron and rudder to make it turn. I never flew for more than fifteen or twenty minutes at a time, but it was kinda fun."

To Lt. Martin, however, this was nothing new. With one hundred hours of flight time vs. Robinson's occasional twenty minutes, it was not surprising that the bombardier had no difficulty in landing the big plane.

The weeks passed as Nelson's crew logged flight after flight. Each man was busy learning his own job, but Lt. Nelson was perhaps the busiest of all. As Airplane Commander, Nelson had to get to know each of his crew members as individuals, and had to evaluate their performance. This meant that in addition to his own flying duties he had to learn their jobs, too. Sgt. Robinson found Nelson's character well suited for command: "Nelson was a fun guy. He was no dyed-in-the-wool officer. He was a soldier. He was just there because he had to be. Nelson wasn't a man to lord his rank over the enlisted men. He was one of the guys. The crew thought the world of him. And Nelson had a lot of concern for the crew. Our welfare was uppermost on his mind. He would ask if we needed anything, and he was very sincere. He always made sure we had money to go into town or whatever. He took good care of us."

Some of the training flights didn't require a full crew. Many of the night missions were navigation and pilot exercises, which gave the gunners time for housekeeping and socializing. Russell Robinson talks about his off duty hours, and his new crewmates: "My wife drove her '40 Mercury to Alexandria. She shared an apartment with Bernice Bartley. The four of us had dinner together a few times. Sometimes I'd take the car and go places with Ron Bartley. He was good company. We'd go out and get things for our wives.

Joe Rex and Carl Moore pose with Ronald and Bernice Bartley and Mauverdene and Russell Robinson in Alexandria, Louisiana, Fall of 1943.

Ten Men

"Carl Moore was a real decent guy. He didn't drink, he didn't smoke, but he was around with the crowd. No hanky panky. He was engaged to a woman named Ellen. Carl had soft drinks when the rest of us were drinking beer, but he had just as good a time as any of us. He was right along with everybody, whatever they wanted to do, but he didn't gamble. I traded him candy bars for cigarettes, because he didn't smoke and I didn't eat candy. I'd trade him candy bars, or other things from our rations if he would iron my shirts and pants, because I really didn't care too much about the housework. Carl was a real nice fella."

"Joe Rex seemed like a real jolly guy. He smoked, but I don't think he drank much. Maybe some beer. Joe was married, too, but his wife wasn't nearby. He went with us on furloughs and 48 hour passes. He was the youngest of us all.

"Mac Hagbo and Tom Sowell ran around together a whole lot. They loved to drink beer together. Mac didn't have much to say. He kept to himself much of the time, but he and Sowell were two of a kind. I can imagine Sowell at the bar, making jokes and drinking beers. And there's Hagbo, just drinking his beer and talking to Tom. Mac was only in the service for one reason, and that's because he was told to go. It didn't make much difference to him. He didn't get too excited about anything.

"That old Tom (Sowell) was hard to beat. He was a character. He was a guy you could never get mad at. He always had a grin on his face about something. He'd do some of the funniest things, and he liked to drink beer. And the more he drank, the funnier he got.

"Archie kept to himself quite a bit. Maybe he was pre-occupied with the job he had. I think that being engineer was something he took pretty seriously. He probably spent more time working with the plane than any of us realized. He might have been out doing that while the rest of us were playing poker.

Archie Mathies photographed his crewmates on October 28, 1943, only days before the men began the trip to England. L to R, top row: Carl Moore, Tom Sowell, Mac Hagbo. L to R, bottom row: Russell Robinson, Joe Rex.

"The officers went off on their own, on leave or on passes. We didn't see much of them. They had more freedom than we had. They could go off base anytime they wanted to, unless they had to fly. Nelson and Truemper went around together some, but I think the officers would have liked to have been with the enlisted men. The enlisted men had more fun.

"Joe Martin wasn't much for socializing with the other crew members, but sometimes he'd go with the officers. He went to town by himself, and came in by himself. We [*enlisted men*] didn't try to force ourselves on him. He seemed to like it that way."

Tom Sowell recalls his impressions of the crew in training. He too found Lt. Martin somewhat distant: "I didn't actually have much to do with Martin. He didn't

Valor at Polebrook

want to associate with us, that's true. He might have been bitter about having been washed out of flying school, but he could still do his job. That's what mattered.

The officers of Nelson's crew as photographed by Archie Mathies. From left, in front - Joe Martin and Walter Truemper. In back - Ronald Bartley and Dick Nelson.

"Russell never had much to say. He'd go out with us, and have a beer once in a while. He went with Joe Rex and Carl Moore sometimes. Russ would do anything as part of the team, and he knew his job.

"Me and Mac Hagbo, we were real close. We went out together all the time. And we'd play poker. Hagbo was a good gambler. I did O.K., too. All told, I won a healthy pot full of money. I sent it all to my mother to put in the bank in my name.

"Joe Rex never did play poker. He preferred pinochle, and we'd all play that sometimes. He might have gone out with Carl or Archie a couple of times, but he didn't much associate with me or Mac 'cause we'd drink beer and gamble.' Joe was real religious. That was important to him, and we respected it. He was a good kid.

"Carl Moore was a straight-laced, religious man. He was quiet in manner, but he had a smile for everyone. Carl'd go out with us once in a while, but he didn't drink. He could still have a good time though."

"Archie was very friendly. He laughed all the time. Never seemed to have a serious thought really, but he knew he had an important job. I don't know that he went out all that much. He spent a lot of time with the plane.

"Lt. Nelson was a fine commander. He was real pleasant and easy going. He wouldn't ask you to do anything he wouldn't do himself. Now Ron Bartley, you couldn't beat him. He just laughed all the time. He was always pulling something, always kidding somebody."

Given the randomness with which the crew was selected, the absence of a "group chemistry" is not surprising. Each crewman found a buddy or two, and small social sets formed among the men, but there weren't any cliques or outcasts. As with Hagbo and Sowell, a strong friendship grew between Nelson and Truemper. Archie Mathies also found a deep respect and admiration for his pilot. Nelson's men got along well together and steadily developed a quiet competence which transcended any social barriers that may have existed in private life.

In Alexandria, Nelson's men had little to distinguish them from the hundreds of other airmen on the base. They had been assigned crew number 58, but they did not have a plane of their own.

Ten Men

Their training flights had been flown in several of the B-17s on the field, and those wore only numbers and code letters. On October 30th, 1943, Crew 58 posed beneath the nose of one of those planes for an official Army Air Force photo. It was the standard setting; the four officers kneeling in the front row, the six enlisted men standing behind them. It was a fitting composition which closely represented the arrangement of the men at their flight stations. (See photo in Dedication.)

Clarence Richard Nelson, pilot and crew leader, smiles for Archie's camera.

Lt. Martin flew up front, separated from the outside air only by the Plexiglas nose through which he aimed his bombsight. Martin would also fire the guns mounted in the turret below the nose. Lt. Truemper's office was a narrow plywood table five feet behind Martin, and to the left. When not calculating position or course, Truemper would also become a gunner. Behind Truemper was the crawlway leading back past the escape hatch below the cockpit. This crawlway opened upward into the cockpit through a rectangular hatch between the pilot's seats. Directly behind the pilots, Carl Moore would stand to operate the top gun turret.

The flight engineer normally flew top turret, but it was best that Sgt. Moore manned the upper guns. Joe Rex explains: "I don't remember any time we took off in that plane that Carl didn't get airsick. I don't know how he kept on flying. He took airsick pills, not every time, but they didn't work very well."

Russell Robinson also knew of Sgt. Moore's problem: "Carl Moore seemed to throw up every time we flew, but he stayed right there. Sometimes we'd be down low and it was hot, and the plane was bouncing all over. It was rough on him. I really have to give him credit. All he had to do was to say, 'I just can't do it. I get sick every time I fly.' There wouldn't have been any disgrace. The pilots knew about it. He was right behind them. He'd turn around and lean into the bomb bay and empty his stomach right there. And he kept right on flying with us."

Joe Rex's radio room was immediately aft of the bomb bay. Rex had the place to himself. It's walls were crowded with racks of transmitters, receivers, and other tools of the radioman's trade. Mounted overhead in an egg-shaped window was the single .50 caliber machine gun Rex would fire to protect against attack from above.

In flight, Archie Mathies would be found curled up in the cramped confines of the ball turret, the first position aft of the radio room. Archie would be half in, half out of the B-17 while he spun and rolled the turret to fire at the enemy. The ball was awkward to climb into and out of. Entry was gained through a removable panel which was accessible only when the ball's guns were pointed straight down. It would be very difficult for Archie to get out in a hurry, should the need arise.

In the tubular fuselage just aft of the ball turret, Tom Sowell and Russell Robinson would stand to fire their guns. A single .50 caliber machine gun was mounted in a sealed window on each side of the plane. Whether looking for enemy fighters or just taking in the scenery below, the two waist gunners would have an excellent view.

Far behind the others, Mac Hagbo would protect their tail with his two .50 caliber guns. Hagbo would be quite isolated from the crew, as he had no direct visual contact due to his location. The intercom was his only link to his shipmates.

From their first day in Alexandria, the rumor mill had been working overtime producing stories of where the men would be sent, and when. In early November, 1943, Lt. Nelson felt certain that deployment could not be long in coming. Mrs. Nelson's journal recalls that time:

"...Dick wrote us that he thought his crew would be leaving for over seas shortly, and asked that Dad and I come down to Alexandria to visit him and meet his crew. We were in Topeka at the time, and decided to drive down. We arrived at Alexandria on Sunday, November 14th, where our pilot and his crew gave us a rousing reception!! After being comfortably settled in our hotel, Dick, Dad and I had dinner together and talked way into the night. The next day and the following, we were together every available moment, and on that Monday evening the crew invited Dad and me to a lovely dinner just outside of Alexandria. While there, Carl Moore, the assistant Engineer, sang with the orchestra, as he has a lovely voice. The boys were happy and carefree, and glad to have a few hours of respite from Army routine. During dinner the boys asked me to name their new plane, which they would be picking up shortly. This was quite a surprise to me, and quite an honor, and I begged time in which to think. After a few moments, the name "MIZPAH" came to me. I told them, and they were especially delighted when I explained that it was a Bible name found in Genesis 31:49, and means "God be with you until we meet again." They accepted gratefully, and felt that being from the Bible, the name alone should protect them.

"On Tuesday the three boys - Dick, Wally Truemper, and Joe Martin - drove as far as Little Rock, Arkansas with Dad and me. The boys went on to Memphis to see May Lane, and Dad and I went on to Topeka. At the station when we bid the boys good-bye, I hugged and kissed them, and said that was from their mothers too. Little we realized this day, Tuesday, November 16th, was the last time we would see our pilot."

During the brief time they spent in Alexandria, Mr. and Mrs. Nelson made a favorable and lasting impression on the crew. Many of "the boys", as Mrs. Nelson called them, felt an immediate fondness for the elder couple. Far from home, and having been away from their own parents for so long, the men were drawn to the warm and caring people who had driven so far to meet them. In the weeks and months

Ten Men

to follow, many of the crew would write to the Nelson's with the same sincerity and openness they shared with their own families.

After a two day stop in Memphis, Dick Nelson and the others returned to Alexandria for the last time. In a letter dated November 19th, Ronald Bartley thanked his sister Juanita for sending Christmas presents to him and Bernice in Alexandria, and mentioned that *"another four or five days and you would have missed us."* Bartley's call was only slightly off. That same day, the Nelson crew boarded a train bound for Kearney, Nebraska. For the first time, the crew would have their own bomber.

B-17G serial number 42-31496 would become home to Nelson's men, and was the plane they were to fly to England. Russell Robinson recalls that this aircraft had very little flight time in its log book: "We finished up in Alexandria about the third week of November, then went by train to Kearney, Nebraska, to pick up our new bomber. That plane didn't have the olive drab paint. It was silver. They were leaving them unpainted by then. We flew the acceptance flights for the Air Force. We had a brand-new plane, and nowhere to go. We were getting familiar with the plane, and we just flew around over Nebraska, into Kansas, out over Colorado. We'd go out for two or three hours, then we'd go back in and land. Lt. Nelson had some of us fly then, too. We stayed in Kearney for about a week, then left for Syracuse, New York."

On November 30th Walter Truemper gave Lt. Nelson an Easterly heading, and their shiny new bomber lifted its wheels from the Midwestern ground for the last time. The flight plan called for an overnight stop in Syracuse, to be followed the next day by a short hop to Bangor, Maine. When navigator Truemper plotted their course prior to the flight, he realized that they would fly almost directly over his home town of Aurora, Illinois.

Walter Truemper was deeply devoted to his mother, Mrs. Friedericka Truemper, who was in poor health and was confined to a wheel chair. Seeing an opportunity for a personal "good-bye" gesture, he instructed his sister Ann to have their mother waiting near the sitting room window at a certain time on the afternoon of the flight. He said Mrs. Truemper would know his plane because it's shadow would fly right into her lap. At the appointed time, Mrs. Truemper was seated at the window. Lt. Truemper's calculations were right on the mark. Nelson guided the ship along the detour his navigator called for. The shadow of the plane moved quickly through the leafless trees, up the long back lawn, and in through the framed glass. Nelson circled around, and the shadow found the navigator's mother again. It filled Mrs. Truemper's heart with joy to have her son so close, and to see how well he did his job. At the same time, she felt a great sadness. Her boy was going to war.

After landing in Syracuse, and receiving more of his crew's travel orders, Lt. Nelson carried out a plan he had devised with his father in Alexandria. A pre-arranged code phrase was included in a telegram to Nelson's parents. The message told them their son was bound for England, and war in Europe. The men were expecting a quick departure from Syracuse, but Sgt. Robinson reports that they had more of an opportunity to see the city than was anticipated: "While we were getting ready to leave Syracuse for Bangor, a jeep with a long whip antenna drove under our left wing and tore a hole in our aileron. The aileron had a metal frame covered with

Valor at Polebrook

fabric, and it was ripped wide open. They had no other aileron on the field, and one had to be flown in. It was four days before we could leave again."

With the new aileron in place, the crew landed in Bangor on December 4th and secured their plane on the ramp. They would stay in Maine for a few days in preparation for a flight to Goose Bay, Labrador, several hundred miles to the North. Some of the enlisted men were posted as sentries, including Robinson: "One night I had guard duty. It was cold. They had big heaters that kept the engines warm, and another that blew into the fuselage of the plane, to keep the equipment and instruments warm. It was comfortable in there, warm enough to sleep if you wanted to. Well, I wasn't actually asleep, but Lt. Nelson came out to the plane. He said there wasn't an officer's club on the base. That was one way we had more freedom than the officers did, because we had more clubs to go to. They could only go to the officer's clubs. They weren't allowed to associate with non-commissioned women. They weren't even allowed to be seen with them. If an officer in an officer's uniform and a WAC in a WAC's uniform were together, there'd be a problem. So there was Nelson and he wanted my clothes! A pair of pants, a shirt, and a jacket! Well, we were about the same size, and I had an extra uniform in my barracks bag on the plane, so I let him borrow my clothes and he went out as an enlisted man. He would have been in trouble if they had caught him. But he wanted to be with the crowd. He was that type of guy."

Both Nelson and Robinson survived that night without incident, and shortly afterward their plane was in the air again, bound for Goose Bay. After an uneventful flight, an equipment malfunction caused a bad landing. Tom Sowell describes the approach: "When we went into Labrador from Bangor, the pilots were checking out the windshield defrosters. One of the defroster motors had gone out, and the inside of the windshield had iced up. We were close to the base, and they had to land, but they couldn't see. They headed on in, but they overshot and landed too far down the runway, which was all ice. The snow that was shoved off to the sides of the runway was piled up real high, and our plane plowed into that sideways. The wheels were packed full of snow and ice. They had to use an engine pre-heater to melt it all out. That didn't hurt the plane, but we had to wait for them to fly in another defroster, and a part for one propeller."

Goose Bay lies at the west end of Lake Melville, a long, tapered body of water which reaches almost ninety miles inland from the Labrador Sea. To Robinson, the flight North hadn't improved their surroundings at all: "Labrador was a desolate, barren place. It was nothing but ice, snow, and a few trees. It was really dreary. I only saw one or two nurses, and lots of those big Eskimo dogs. We were told not to bother the dogs. They weren't too friendly. I got up one morning and looked out the window. It had snowed during the night, and there were big mounds of snow here and there. And under each one of those mounds was a sleeping dog.

"There wasn't much to do. We mostly just stayed in the barracks. It was too dang cold, anyway, around twenty below zero. We were there for nine or ten days, waiting for some other planes and some equipment."

The "other planes" were a group of B-17s with which Nelson's crew would be

Ten Men

crossing the North Atlantic. Their destination was Prestwick, Scotland, over 2,000 miles to the East. The fuel load necessary for so long a flight would allow a cruise speed of only 160 miles per hour. The crew could expect a flight time of almost fourteen hours.

By December 14th all was ready for the group's departure. The crew's barracks bags and flight rations were taken aboard, along with some unofficial "cargo". Having been rather successful at the card table, Sergeants Hagbo and Sowell had spent their winnings on candy, cigarettes, and liquor. This contraband was secured in the aft fuselage, where it would attract little attention.

As engines were started and the crews made their ships ready for takeoff, Sgt. Robinson could not know that the coming flight would frighten him more than some of his later combat missions: "It was dark when we left, and there were nine planes in our group. We didn't try to fly formation. Each plane was kind of on its own. We might have been a half a mile apart. I never did see any of them, but over the radio we could hear other planes talking back and forth all night. It wasn't far out from Labrador that we ran into weather we didn't expect. It was foggy, and misty. I couldn't see the sky.

"My main job then was to stand at the right waist window and watch the wing. I could see the ice building up. The light from the cabin would shine out, and I could see the props turning. When the ice got thick, I'd tell the pilots, and they'd activate the deicer boots on the leading edges of the wings. The boots would inflate and break the ice, and big sheets would come loose and blow back across the wing.

"Ice also built up on the props. They used glycol to de-ice the props. When the chunks of ice tore loose from the prop blades, they'd hit the sides of the plane, right up there by the pilots. They didn't come through, but they made big dents in the skin, and a hell of a racket."

The ice caused more trouble than just noise and a few dents in the skin. Robinson explains: "We didn't have a full load of oxygen on board that flight, and if we stayed down at an altitude where we didn't need oxygen, we'd ice up. So we'd climb above the weather to get rid of the ice, but then we'd be using our oxygen too fast. So, we'd come back down to conserve oxygen. But then we'd get more ice, and we'd have to climb again. Just up and down, up and down."

While the ice and oxygen dilemma was a serious problem, Robinson could not see the other force acting against the plane. Unknown to him, an unusually strong headwind had slowed their ground speed to a crawl. They were burning fuel faster than they were crossing the ocean. Sgt. Robinson continues: "The officers got to talking that we had to make a decision pretty quick, because we were approaching the point of no return. If we went much further, we wouldn't have enough gas to get back to Goose Bay, and if we went on we wouldn't have enough gas to get to Scotland, because of the wind."

With their survival at stake, Lt. Nelson decided to turn around while they could still return to Labrador. This was welcome news to the crew, but Tom Sowell says the pilot's choice created a different problem for him: "We got a third of the way over, and we'd used half our gas, and were still buckin' that headwind. So we turned around and headed back to Goose Bay, but we still wondered if we would make it. Then Lt. Truemper came back by us and said, 'Lt. Nelson says to jettison everything. Pull

Valor at Polebrook

whatever we don't need and throw it overboard.' Then he asked me 'Tom, what about that whiskey and those cigarettes?' And I said, 'Well, you don't need to worry about that. Me, Hagbo, and Davey Jones will deliberate that one.' And he left it to us. 'Course I expect he knew there was no way that stuff was going to end up in Davey Jones' locker at the bottom of the ocean."

Nelson and Bartley battled wind, ice, and the fuel gauges for several more hours, but eventually made it back to Labrador. It was a tired and relieved crew that climbed out of their cold-soaked airplane.

On December 16th, the group tried again. This time their destination was a U.S. airfield in Nuts Corner, Ireland. Sgt. Sowell was pleased to find the winds more cooperative the second time, but still couldn't seem to get across the ocean without something going wrong: "Two days later we took off again with the same candy, cigarettes, and booze. We headed out over the ocean, and a bunch of us were in the radio room playing pinochle with Joe Rex. After a while, Trump came back with us, too. He'd look up out the radio room bubble, to see the stars, and every so often he'd get on the intercom and say, 'Hey, Dick, take so many degrees left or right,' like he was doing celestial navigation just by taking a glance. Later Lt. Nelson called back, "Trump, where are you taking us?" And Trump said, "I'm taking us to England, where we'll quickly put an end to this war."

"That was a long flight, and the next morning I had gotten deathly sick and had to use the airsick bucket to vomit in. We were landing in Ireland and I was still leaning over that bucket when Lt. Nelson hit the runway. When the tail wheel came down, the mess in that bucket came up around me. As soon as we stopped I got out and stood in the rain at the side of the airplane and took a bath. And boy, that was a cold rain."

Sgt. Sowell would discover that in England bad weather was more common than sunshine, and that he would again feel the numbing chill of the winter rain.

Sergeants dressed for war. Kneeling, left to right - Joe Rex, Archie Mathies, Carl Moore. Standing, left to right - Tom Sowell, Russell Robinson, Mac Hagbo. Fall, 1943.

Chapter Two: England

Sometime, somewhere, during the Army Air Force's exodus to England, someone started the tradition of the "short-snorter". Just as graduating seniors would sign each other's high-school annual, airmen would exchange signatures on pieces of paper money in the currency of each country over which they flew. A flier's collection would grow as successive missions took him over new territory.

On December 17th, the men of Nelson's crew signed their first short-snorters. Ronald Bartley passed around a two-dollar bill. It soon carried the signatures of Nelson's crew, and of other men who had been in the group on the flight over. Russell Robinson's George Washington received similar honors and was returned to his wallet for safekeeping. The signing of the short-snorters marked a turning point for these young fliers as they traveled to go into battle. The terrible purpose which brought their names together would change their lives forever. All of the signatures would return home. Some of the men would not.

In the chill of mid-December, with Christmas only a week away, Nelson and crew faced another layover at an army airfield. Russell Robinson had time to start learning about life in the British Isles: "We were in Nut's Corner two or three days. The British were working on the airbase there. We gave them some of our cigarettes. We had a bunch of them. We carried ten cases of cigarettes (in addition to Sowell's booty) on the trip, because it was a fast way to get them over there. The British didn't have the best cigarettes in the world, and they were glad to get ours.

"We could go by truck into Belfast, to dance, and to drink beer. Of course, Belfast was all blacked out. When we got into town, there were these kids waiting at the bus stop. We'd give them a shilling, or two shillings, and they'd lead us to the clubs, NCO clubs, or Red Cross places, or whatever, because we couldn't find them. And then, when we had to get back to the base, they'd be waiting outside of the clubs, and we'd have to give them more money to take us back to the bus. We couldn't find our way around by ourselves.

"On the night we were supposed to leave Ireland, one of the guys was late getting back to the base. We had to lay over an extra night. And that night, we had a big windstorm. The planes were out on the pads where they parked them, but they weren't tied down. The wind went whipping through there, and it was awful strong. It just spun those planes around, and pushed the tails of some planes into the wings and fuselages of the others. Three bombers were damaged, and ours was one of them. Well, we couldn't fly out of Ireland, so they put us on a boat for Glasgow, Scotland. We loaded the next evening, when it was

Valor at Polebrook

getting dark. We were climbing up the gangplank, to get onto the top deck, and at the same time there were cows and sheep being loaded down below. We headed out across the North Channel and up the Firth of Clyde. It was about a four-hour trip. We didn't have anything to eat because it wasn't a regular passenger ship, but there were things to drink. We didn't worry about torpedoes. Maybe we should have, but at night, with no lights on the ship or on the land, we couldn't even tell we were on water. Once in a while we could feel the ship raise up under our feet, then go back down again, and feel the floating a little bit, but that was all. When we got to Scotland we had to lay over in Glasgow for about ten hours while we waited for a train to England. When we got off the train we went to a staging area to find out where to go next."

Robinson and the others would find themselves in several "staging areas" during the weeks to follow. The process of sending men and aircraft over to England was a monumental task. With hundreds of bombers making the Atlantic crossing each month, the Army had an unending job in keeping track of the new arrivals and assigning them to bases and barracks. As the airwar continued, losses of airmen and bombers created a constant demand for replacements of each. The Army's solution to this logistics nightmare was to set up a "warehouse" system, where people and airplanes became inventory in a giant stockroom of airbases and training centers. Incoming aircraft were inspected and given necessary repairs or maintenance. After being brought up to combat flying status, they were put into the aircraft pool. When needed, the bombers were flown to operational airfields. The planes did not sit idle for long.

Incoming crews required fine-tuning as well. Their stateside training had taught them the technical aspects of their jobs, but the men still had much to learn before going on combat missions. Pilots, navigators, bombardiers, radiomen, and gunners all required training in the specifics of making war in the skies over Europe. Everything from finding their home airfields to flying in large formations had to be explained, learned, and understood. New crews would benefit from the experience of veteran fliers, but the urgent need for replacements left little time for schooling.

Soon after arriving in England, the Nelson crew was assigned to the Eighth Air Force Replacement Depot Casual Pool, First Replacement and Training Squadron. The officers were sent for advanced instruction in their respective trades. Sgt. Joe Rex had to learn radio procedures, call signs, frequencies, and numerous other details of the combat radioman's job. As flight engineer, Sgt. Mathies had the additional responsibility of learning to work with the aircraft maintenance system and ground crews. His first weeks in England kept him fully occupied.

The four remaining Sergeants were sent to AAF Station 172, the First Combat Crew Gunnery Center, in the town of Snettisham. Located almost ninety miles due north of London, Snettisham is two miles inland on the Eastern Shore of an almost perfectly square bay known as The Wash. The bay is nearly ten miles long on each side, a perfect place for machine gun and artillery practice. At Snettisham, Russell Robinson found visible evidence of the war he and his crewmates would soon be joining: "One of the first places we went for training was called The Wash. That was

England

on the coast. There was an old summer resort, and they had made a gunnery range out of it. We could see where the beaches had been mined at one time. When the British expected to be invaded, they mined most of their shoreline. After they knew they wouldn't be invaded they went out and dug up the mines. Some were intentionally set off. That left a lot of pits and craters on the beaches.

"The Wash was a dreary place. It was winter, and it was windy and damp most of the time. There were all these gunners there, but we didn't know anyone except our own crew. Gunnery school was more monotonous than anything, but we had to know how to shoot those fifty calibers. The main thing was to learn how to hit the target. And we had aircraft identification. We had to know what we were shooting at. We had to learn German planes, and Japanese too, because they were on the same side. And we had to know the American planes so we wouldn't shoot at our own guys.

"They had a ball turret set up on a stand. We could take some training in that if we wanted too, so I did. I never did fly the ball. I didn't like that position. It was really cramped. You flew with your knees almost up around your head because you couldn't stretch out. The two gun handles were in between your legs and you sighted through a round window between your feet. It was really uncomfortable in there, and it got cold too, especially if your electric suit stopped heating. I didn't care to ride down there at all.

"Another thing I didn't like about gunnery school was that we were hungry most of the time because we couldn't get very good food. They just didn't have much to eat in the English towns nearby, unless you went to the USO, or the Red Cross, but they did have fish and chips. Boy, those were good. The English people were awfully good to us. Sometimes they'd feed us in their homes. We tried to compensate them. We'd take them whatever we could get for them, things they were short on. It wasn't ever much, but they appreciated it."

Archie Mathies' duty station: the ball turret. (Photo by Jeff Rogers)

Valor at Polebrook

Christmas came and went with the scattered crew enjoying the holiday as best they could under the circumstances. Flight Officer Bartley resumed his letter writing, excusing his lag in correspondence by blaming the censors who wouldn't let him say anything specific about where he was or what he had seen on the trip over. In a letter to his sister Juanita, dated December 30, 1943, Ronald explained that his family would have to wait for the details of his travels. He summed up all that had happened since leaving the States by writing, *"I had a great trip over here, and a very enjoyable Christmas day, with turkey and all the trimmings. Spent the rest of the day quietly on the base..."*

Like all servicemen overseas, Ronald Bartley could only stay in touch with his wife and family members through a continuous exchange of letters.

1943 ended, 1944 began, and little else changed for the men of Nelson's crew. Their training continued despite the dreary weather. On the few days when the clouds lifted, groups of heavy bombers could be seen forming up overhead. The four sergeants wondered how long it would be until they were on one of the planes they were watching. On January 19th, the Army assigned Nelson's men to operational duty with the 510th Bomb Squadron, 351st Bomb Group (H). Within days the crew was re-united at their new home: Polebrook.

Polebrook airfield lies seventy miles north and slightly west of London, near the large town of Peterborough. It was originally known as RAF Polebrook, having been built in late 1940 and early 1941 for RAF Bomber Command. Some of the first aircraft to be operated from Polebrook were early B-17s supplied to Britain. These aircraft (designated "Fortress I" by the RAF) suffered so badly in combat that they were withdrawn from operational duties and used in training and liaison roles. The British also operated B-24s from Polebrook, but not for combat purposes.

Early in 1942, when arrangements were being made to base U.S. bombers in England, Polebrook's runways were lengthened and additional hardstands were built. In June, Polebrook became headquarters for the 97th Bomb Group, the first USAAF unit to arrive in England. Two squadrons of B-17Es were stationed at Polebrook, and it was from this airfield that the first Eighth Air Force bombing mission was flown on August 17th. In October of 1942 the 97th was transferred to duty in the Mediterranean Theater, leaving Polebrook unoccupied until the 351st arrived early in 1943.

By January of 1944, the 351st was an experienced outfit, despite being barely

England

over a year old. The Group was formed in November of 1942, and was comprised of the 508th, 509th, 510th, and 511th Bomb Squadrons. The first Group Commander was Lt. Col. William A. Hatcher. After organization and training in the States, the 351st departed for England. Between May 13th and December 31st, 1943, Colonel Hatcher lead or directed the 351st through 66 missions. When Col. Hatcher was shot down and captured on the December 31st mission, Colonel Eugene Romig was assigned as his replacement. Romig, a West Point graduate, had commanded the 359th squadron of the 303rd Bomb Group, another B-17 unit based at Molesworth, ten miles south of Polebrook. In February of 1943, Romig became the 303rd Group Operations Officer and was promoted to Lieutenant Colonel. Romig took command of the 351st in the first week of January 1944.

Polebrook airfield, home of the 351st Bomb Group. The control tower and field recognition square are just to the left of center, near the "J" shaped driveway. The bare-metal B-17s on the runways and hardstands date this photo to mid-1944 or later.

Valor at Polebrook

When Nelson's crew reached Polebrook late in the third week of January, they found the unusual arrangement of having the barracks, mess hall, bathing, and recreational facilities separated from the main base by a wide expanse of forest. The men quickly settled into their quarters however, as it took very little time to unpack their few, basic possessions. The crew did not go immediately into combat. Bad weather during the last weeks of January allowed only four missions to be flown between the 21st and the 30th, and the men found themselves with a little more free time than they had expected. Flight Officer Bartley took the chance to get back to letter writing. Excerpts from his January 27th letter to his sister Mary tell their own story: *"I received your letter today, the one written Dec. 27. It took exactly a month. Of course, the next one won't take that long as it won't have as much chasing around to do to catch me. Your letter is the first I have received since I came over here, so maybe you can imagine how happy I was to get it. I hope one of Bernice's comes through soon.*

"I'm terribly sorry I couldn't be there to get the present you had fixed up for me. Just hang on to it for a while, and maybe I'll be back soon to get it. Well, by next Christmas anyway. HA!

"I missed sending my laundry out today, so I may have to do it myself tomorrow. I can do it, too!

"This is a heck of a nice base. Everything is O.K., even the mud! Write soon. Love, Ronny."

As a newcomer among men who were already flying missions, Russell Robinson found the atmosphere of a combat barracks very different from others he had occupied: "We had six crews of six enlisted men in each barracks. The officers had their quarters nearby. We didn't bunk with them. Each crew had it's space in the barracks, an army cot and foot locker for each man. It sure wasn't anything fancy. We had coke stoves for heat, and sometimes that wasn't enough. It got cold in England, cold and damp.

Domestic chores at Polebrook. Tom Sowell (left), Mac Hagbo (leaning over table at left), Carl Moore, and an airman named Alec use gasoline to clean their flying clothes.

"Whenever a crew went down, there were six men gone out of the barracks. Sometimes two crews out of the same barracks. It really looked empty then. We never knew what happened to crewmen who didn't come back, and the Army didn't give out the particulars. If another crew saw a plane go down, they might say, 'We saw six chutes', or 'ten chutes', but we could never be sure what happened to the guys."

Sometimes the men were issued passes, which allowed them to venture into nearby English towns in search of "recreation". One such place was Oundle, a country crossroads town two miles west of the airbase, where the Rose and Crown pub became a favorite gathering place for off-duty airmen. Farther away, but much

England

larger than Polebrook or Oundle, was Peterborough. It did not take long for Tom Sowell to begin exploring this new neighborhood: "Peterborough was a pretty good sized town. There was a bus that went right downtown. It was about a thirty-minute ride from the base. The Red Cross had a place there. We could play cards, and get a little food, and they'd likely buy coffee and doughnuts. They always wanted us to sign the register, so they'd know where we were if an emergency came up. We'd go try out the different pubs. The English women didn't go into the bars much, just the men. But a whole bunch of girls would walk the streets. They were the Land Army girls, who'd cut wood and trim roadways, and whatever. They slept in the cattle barns on straw mattresses. Those girls did hard work. They took care of the land."

Occasionally, England took care of the men too, or perhaps it took advantage of them. Russell Robinson explains: "One time, after a night in Peterborough, Sowell, Hagbo, me, and some others missed the bus. There were no more busses going back. If you missed the last bus, you were going to walk. But we found a taxi, and the driver said he'd take us back to Polebrook. Back at the base, when it was time to pay the fare, we didn't know how to count English money. I don't know how much we gave that old boy that night. We just had to take his word for it that it was the right amount."

Russell Robinson, Archie Mathies, and Carl Moore. Hastily constructed, the barracks at Polebrook provided only basic protection against the English climate.

The Red Lion, a pub in nearby Oundle, provided a gathering place for off-duty servicemen from several bases.

Valor at Polebrook

Early February saw the weather improve enough to allow a series of missions to be flown from Polebrook but the Nelson crew was not yet assigned an aircraft. Joe Martin was called to substitute for another bombardier on one occasion. Archie Mathies also made a fill in-flight. Apart from these two, the men stayed on the ground. During this interval, Dick Nelson began to look around for an artist who could paint the word "Mizpah" on ten relatively new leather flying jackets. Nelson felt that even if his men didn't have their own plane, they should have an identity as a crew.

On February 5th Colonel Romig himself lead a mission to Chateauroux, France, where aircraft hangars and runways were bombed with good results. Then, on the sixth, Nelson and crew got the call to go. The Mission Leader that day was Major Elzia Ledoux, the Commanding Officer of the 509th squadron. An experienced flier and leader, Ledoux began pilot training in December of 1940. After receiving his wings in August of 1941, his first assignment was to Orlando, Florida, where he flew B-18s and B-25s. In January of 1942, Ledoux transferred to the 34th Bomb Group in Portland, Oregon, the unit from which the 351st's original officers were selected. Major Ledoux commanded the 509th from it's beginning, and by war's end he would bear the distinction of having lead his squadron through one stretch of 54 missions without losing an aircraft. Ledoux would also play a crucial part in the fate of Lt. Nelson's crew.

The February sixth mission was a strike against another target in France. The flight was not a long one but Flight Officer Bartley did not accompany his shipmates on the raid. Standard procedure called for new crews to fly with an experienced pilot on their first mission. For this reason, Lt. Nelson flew as copilot in aircraft 42-38038, a B-17 named "April Girl II". Another 510th Squadron pilot, Lt. Harold M. Peters, sat in the left seat. Nelson and crew felt a mixture of excitement and fear as they climbed into the aircraft. They had heard stories of good missions and bad ones. There was no way to know which they would have that day.

Sergeant Bartholomew Hagan of the 508th squadron was the left waist gunner in "Yankee Rebel", the lead ship of the formation on the February 6th raid. An entry in his war diary describes the mission that introduced Nelson's crew to combat:

Archie Mathies, wearing the insulated leather flying suit needed to protect against the intense cold at high altitudes.

England

"We were lead ship of the composite group today. Lt. Floden was pilot. This was the furthest into France I have gone to date. We expected it to be pretty rough as we were going in at 14,000 feet. Assembly was good and we took off across the channel okay. There were hundreds of P-38s and P-47s most of the way in. There was a pretty heavy overcast so we couldn't see the target. Had no PFF (radar equipped pathfinder aircraft) with us, so we did not bomb. Hit some light flak on the way home. Near the coast we sighted an airfield so chose it as a last resort target. There was a good pattern and I saw two hangers blown sky high. P-51s picked us up at the coast and took us home. No enemy fighters were sighted. More of a joy ride than a raid."

Tom Sowell agreed with Sgt. Hagan. Sowell's first taste of combat left him unimpressed: "Our first mission was a milk-run. There wasn't nothin' to it. I came back and walked into the barracks, and I said, 'Shoot, you people ain't got no sweat. You got one damn war over here, and all you need is one Texan to win it. The rest of y'all can go home.'" Sgt. Sowell would feel differently after his second mission.

Aircraft of the 351st Bomb Group dodge flak enroute to the target.

Valor at Polebrook

Twenty-four planes flew the group's 80th mission by paying a visit to Frankfurt on February 11, but Nelson's crew was not among them. Bombs were dropped through the overcast. Breaks in the clouds allowed some crewmembers to observe hits in the target area. The escorting fighters kept German opposition at bay. One B-17 was hit over the target and landed in enemy territory. Another crew was forced to crash-land in England. Those men were able to exit the plane before it burned.

After four consecutive flyable days, bad weather returned on February 12th. 351st Group activity during the next seven days is described in a diary kept by Staff Sergeant Edgar Matlock. Matlock was an attorney in civilian life, and could have been an officer, but he preferred to serve as an enlisted man in the Operations office of the 510th squadron. His entries for the week are as follows:

Feb. 12 - The weather was unfavorable today. There was some local flying.

Feb. 13 - The weather was poor again today. There was a large practice mission scheduled for this afternoon, but even it had to be scrubbed.

Feb. 14 - The combat mission scheduled for today was scrubbed one hour before briefing. There was no flying done by our squadron. Weather was unfavorable.

Feb. 15 - The combat mission scheduled for today was scrubbed before briefing.

Feb. 16 - There was a loading last night for a combat mission today, however the mission was scrubbed early this morning. We are to have a big inspection tomorrow by Colonel Romig, our Group Commander, so everyone is busy policing up.

Feb. 17 - Another loading came in last night for a combat mission today, however this one was scrubbed this morning before breakfast time. There was no flying done at our base today, due to a heavy overcast and poor visibility.

Feb. 18 - There was an overcast all day and it rained at intervals. We had the inspectors from the First Division with us today and everything turned out O.K. There was no flying done by our squadron today.

Feb. 19 - It was still overcast today, coupled with scattered showers. There was no activity in the air at our base, however they were busy swinging the compasses in our airplanes.

The entries in Edgar Matlock's diary are significant because they provide clues to what was going on behind the scenes at Polebrook and at Eighth Air Force Headquarters. The "large practice mission" scheduled on the 13th, along with the inspection by First Division, were not just intended to help the men pass the time while waiting for the weather to clear up. Col. Romig knew his base had to be in perfect order for the visitors on the 18th, and planned his own inspection accordingly. When the weather did improve, the 351st and the rest of the Eighth Air Force would be very busy indeed.

From the onset of U.S. bomber operations over Europe it was clear that the Liberators and Fortresses could not adequately defend themselves against attacks by German fighters. On short-range missions, Allied fighters could escort the bombers and offer some protection. On longer flights, the bomber formations were left on their own when the escorting

England

fighters ran low on fuel and had to turn back for England. After the disastrous losses during the Schweinfurt missions in August and October 1943, Eighth Air Force HQ planned a series of massive attacks against the Luftwaffe itself. It was hoped that by repeatedly striking at German aircraft factories, production could be slowed or halted, thereby denying the Luftwaffe the planes it needed to continue attacks against the bombers. The plan was logical, but would not be easy to carry out. The factories were deep inside the German homeland. The bomber formations would be subjected to attacks by flak and fighters along almost the entire route of each mission. The Bomb Groups would require a stretch of good weather if the concentrated air-strikes were to be effective, but winter returned to the European continent before the assault could be launched. HQ waited, and watched the weather reports for the first sign of a chance to strike. Officially designated "Operation Argument", these raids would come to be known as The Big Week. It was for this effort that Romig and First Division had to ensure the readiness of the 351st.

Although grounded by unfavorable weather conditions, the Group was not idle during the stand down. Mechanics continued the unending maintenance and repair work needed to keep the B-17s airworthy. Test flights were carried out through broken cloud cover. These "slow time" flights were necessary to test engines and other systems after repair or replacement. A typical flight lasted two to four hours, depending on the items to be checked. The pilots could fly anywhere they chose, but they had to stay over England. Gunners were not usually carried on slow time flights, but an engineer, navigator, and radio operator were required.

The 351st, armed and airborne.

Edgar Matlock's diary does not mention the slow time flight that Nelson and part of his crew logged in mid-February. For some reason, Sgt. Rex was not available for the flight. Another radioman, Technical Sergeant Elmer F. Ruschman, had to stand in for him. Sgt. Ruschman describes the day he flew with Nelson's crew: "On February 18th, 1944, I was in my barracks writing letters to family and friends, as I did almost every chance I got. Around noon, or a little after, one of the men who usually woke us up for missions came in and said that they needed a radio-operator to fly on a slow time job. This would be a four-hour ride over England to break in a new engine before taking the plane into combat. Lt. Nelson, his copilot, navigator, engineer, and another man were in the front end of the plane. I was not too familiar with Nelson's crew, but Carl Moore used to come into our barracks often, and I knew Archie Mathies a little. Whenever I flew with a crew on this type of flight I never went up front unless the pilot would want me for some reason. I was alone in the radio room.

"It was rather cloudy weather, but as we flew for a while there were patches of sunshine over parts of England. It seemed

Valor at Polebrook

as though we had flown a long time. Not a word was said over the intercom. I remember seeing the coastline at various times, and I had the feeling that we were pretty far down in southern England. I knew we had been up for more than four hours and finally navigator Truemper asked me to get a position fix for him. This meant for me to call three ground-radio stations asking them to plot our signal while we flew. They could tell us where we were located. Wherever we were, it was too late to return to Polebrook before dark, and we had to land at an English base and stay overnight. The next day, the 19th, we flew from that base back to Polebrook. When we landed, officials met us, and the officers were questioned as to why we did not return the day before. This did not concern the enlisted men, and we were allowed to go on our way."

Nelson, Bartley, and Truemper were able to explain their actions satisfactorily, as no reprimand was forthcoming. After straightening out the mix-up, the officers returned to their barracks. Later that evening Sgt. Robinson showed up and a pinochle game ensued. Sgt. Mathies joined the game, which lasted for some time. The card-players snacked on sandwiches from the mess hall, while others from the crew wrote letters or caught up on housework. In the relaxed atmosphere of the barracks, thoughts about combat didn't seem to interfere with their leisure time. Maybe they would fly the next day. Maybe they wouldn't. If they did, the men would be up early, and would be in the air before midmorning. If they didn't, they'd go to church and have breakfast together. Either way, it didn't matter on that Saturday night. After a while, the letters were written and set aside for the censors, the card game ended, and the men turned in for the night.

While Nelson and crew had been making their way back to Polebrook, Operations officers at Eighth Air Force Headquarters were assessing the latest weather information. Changes in conditions over the continent indicated that although the cloud cover would persist, some clearing would allow the visibility needed to assure accurate strikes on German aircraft factories. By 2000 hours on February 19th, Col. Romig and other Group commanders had received orders for the mission to be flown the next day. In operations rooms all across East Anglia, typewriters clattered through the early morning hours to relay details of the coming raid. Sunday, February 20th, would be the beginning of The Big Week.

Chapter Three: Mission 81

For the crews scheduled to fly that day, February 20th began with the wake-up call given at 0300. In the darkened barracks, with the coal fires burned almost completely out, the fliers felt the penetrating chill of the damp winter morning. Without looking outside they knew that when the sun came up it would be hidden by low, scudding clouds. They also knew that bad weather over Polebrook would not automatically scrub the mission. If the target was expected to be clear, they would go. One by one, the men rubbed the sleep from their eyes and began to dress for war.

The mess hall began serving breakfast at 0400. In the chow line, Flight Officer Bartley met up with another new copilot, Flight Officer Jack Seagraves. The two had been classmates in flight school and had become friends. Seagraves recalls that Bartley was eager to talk: "My first mission had been to France, on February 5th, but Ron hadn't flown yet. He was very interested in what I had to say about combat. I told him it wasn't too bad, just a little scary when we saw the enemy fighters, and when we were in the flak area. I tried to assure him that he would be all right."

Flight Officer Ronald E. Bartley, on furlough after completing pilot training.

After breakfast, the airmen gathered in the briefing hut to find out where they would be going. The 351st was to provide aircraft and crews for strikes against two objectives. Twenty planes would join squadrons from the 91st and 381st Bomb Groups and fly against targets in Oschersleben, Germany. Another twenty

Valor at Polebrook

A 351st B-17 waits to receive its bomb load. The ground crews were the unsung heroes of every mission.

Mission 81

planes would form the low box of a formation heading for aircraft factories in Leipzig, roughly eighty miles south of Berlin. Nelson's crew was assigned to the Leipzig strike. Russell Robinson remembers that the morning's briefing was typical of every mission: "The whole crew went to the main briefing. There was a curtain on one wall, and when it was pulled back we could see the route to the target plotted out on a big, five foot by six foot map. The briefing officer talked about the target and where the flak and fighters would be. Then the weather officer would talk."

Although the weather report told of improvements in flying conditions at high altitude, there were few signs of change close to the ground. Like many of the preceding days, February 20th was dismal and dreary with temperatures in the mid-thirties. A solid overcast at 3,000 feet threatened to drop more rain, and possibly snow, on the already sodden ground. Pilots would have four mile visibility during the take-off run but would be flying blind the instant they entered the clouds. From bases all across East Anglia, hundreds of aircraft would become airborne within a few minutes of each other. Mid-air collisions were a very real danger.

The marginal weather conditions could play a significant role in the success or failure of the mission. The thick cloud layer extended eastward to cover most of the European continent, but reconnaissance planes had observed breaks in the overcast. Radar equipped "pathfinder" aircraft would be used to locate the German industrial centers electronically, but the targets would have to be visually identified before the bombs were released. The group would strike alternate targets if the primaries could not be found through breaks in the clouds.

When the weather officer completed his portion of the briefing, the crews split up. Pilots, navigators and bombardiers attended additional briefings. The enlisted men went to pick up their weapons and install them in their planes. Once the guns were mounted and loaded, there was little for the men to do until the officers arrived. This gave the rookie airmen time to think about the mission they were about to fly. The February 6th raid into France had taken less than five hours. The Leipzig flight would last almost twice that long. The group would assemble over Deenethorpe, seven miles northwest of Polebrook. Then they would face a six hundred and fifty mile flight across occupied Europe and into Germany. The route was planned to avoid known concentrations of flak, but there would be no avoiding the Luftwaffe. Fighter attacks were expected to be persistent and heavy. P-51s were assigned to escort the formations to the target area, or to the limit of the fighters' endurance. RAF Spitfires would fly out to their maximum combat radius to meet the returning bombers. P-47s would patrol in search of stragglers, and several squadrons of P-38s would be in action over the continent. All told, more than five hundred single and twin engine fighters would be sent out to protect the bombers.

For self-defense, each B-17 carried 9,000 rounds of .50 caliber ammunition. German pilots had a healthy respect for the heavily armed Fortresses, but gunfire would be useless against flak. With many important industrial plants in the city, Leipzig was heavily surrounded by anti-aircraft batteries. Though clouds might hide the target, they would not protect the bombers from flak. Some of the anti-aircraft guns were radar guided, but all of the ground gunners could depend on

Valor at Polebrook

Luftwaffe pilots to report the altitude, heading and speed of the American formations. Armed with this knowledge, the flak gunners' defensive fire could be accurate and deadly. Mission 81 would be no "milk run".

By 0835 Nelson and the other officers had joined the enlisted men on the concrete hardstand where their assigned aircraft was parked. Serial number 42-31763 was one of the last G model B-17s to be painted in the olive-drab-over-grey color scheme. It was equipped with a chin turret but retained the factory tail and non-staggered waist gun positions. '763 had been named Ten Horsepower, although history did not record who had so christened the bomber or if any artwork adorned its nose. On the aft fuselage were painted the squadron code letters "TU", followed by the aircraft letter "A". On the upper right wing and on both sides of the tail, a white triangle framed a black letter "J", the identification mark of the 351st. With five missions already in its log books, Ten Horsepower had seen more combat than the men it would soon carry into battle.

At 0845, from the observation deck of Polebrook's control tower, Major Elzia Ledoux fired the flare that was the signal to start engines. In every cockpit, pilots and copilots smoothly moved through the procedures which would bring the Group's aircraft to life. Ten minutes were allotted for the twenty planes to start up, taxi along the perimeter track, and get into assigned order for take-off. Ten Horsepower was to be the fifteenth plane off. With checklists complete and four engines running, Nelson signaled "all ready" to the ground crew. The chocks were pulled. Ten Horsepower slowly rolled forward to taxi out to the runway.

What happened next is not exactly clear. One story is that, for some unexplained reason, a jeep was driving along the perimeter track. Just as Ten Horsepower began to taxi, the jeep cut in front of the heavily loaded B-17. Nelson, not wanting to dump the plane on its nose by jamming on the brakes, swerved to avoid colliding with the jeep. The plane's right main wheel went off the edge of the taxiway. Under the weight of 2,110 gallons of fuel and 42 one-hundred pound bombs, the wheel burrowed deeply into the water-soaked turf. Nelson applied power in an attempt to pull the big bomber back onto the hardstand. His efforts were futile. Ten Horsepower was stuck in the mud.

B-17s on the perimeter track at Polebrook airfield. The heavily loaded planes rolled smoothly along the concrete taxiway, but would quickly bog down in the soft ground to either side.

The presence of the jeep cannot be verified but, regardless of how it happened, Ten Horsepower was undeniably up to its right axle in trouble. The planes on the taxi-way behind '763 were able to maneuver around the stranded bomber but the take-off order was disrupted. Nelson and crew watched as, one by one, the other planes turned onto the main runway and throttled up. Every thirty seconds, another

A Limited Edition Dedicated to the Valiant Men who Flew on the Epic Last Flight of "Ten Horsepower," a B-17G Flying Fortress from the 351st Bomb Group, 510th Bomb Squadron. The Most Highly Decorated Aircrew in the Eighth Air Force.

VALOR AT POLEBROOK
By David B. Poole

Valor at Polebrook
Published from an original
oil painting by
David B. Poole

Edition limited to 500
artist-signed and numbered
prints each individually
countersigned by three
surviving members of the
aircrew and the Tower
Officer of the Day,
Polebrook Airfield

Overall size 32¼x23½ inches
Image size 27½x17¾ inches
Price $125

SPOFFORD HOUSE

VALOR AT POLEBROOK
By David B. Poole

A Limited Edition Art Print Countersigned by Three Surviving Aircrew Members and the Tower Officer of the Day, Polebrook Airfield

David Poole's painting, "Valor at Polebrook," was inspired by the courageous achievements of the men who became the most highly decorated aircrew in the annals of the Eighth Air Force.

In February 1944, on the opening day of the historic "Big Week" bombing campaign, ten young Americans took off in a B-17 named "Ten Horsepower." It was on a mission to Liepzig, Germany, that they would be thrust into a series of harrowing events that would test their courage almost beyond human comprehension.

The epic story of "Ten Horsepower" and her extraordinary crew is a fascinating account of one of the most unusual experiences of the air war in Europe.

Over the target, they encountered intense flak and ferocious fighter opposition. The co-pilot was killed by a burst that shattered the cockpit area, wounding the pilot so badly that he was rendered unconscious, incapable of flying the aircraft. Miraculously, the top turret gunner, by sheer strength of will, forced his way into the left seat and brought the crippled aircraft under some semblance of control. Now the problem was how to get the crippled "Ten Horsepower," without a pilot, back safely to her home base at Polebrook, England.

Poole's painting shows the valiant "Ten Horsepower," being assisted by a second B-17, as she approaches her ultimate destiny at Polebrook Airfield. A brochure that tells the full story in greater detail accompanies each print in this fine limited edition.

The Signatories:
Sgt. Joseph F. Rex, Radio Operator.
Sgt. Thomas R. Sowell, Left Waistgunner.
Sgt. Russell R. Robinson, Right Waistgunner
Major Elzia Ledoux, Tower Officer of the Day.

Valor at Polebrook
Edition limited to 500 artist-signed numbered prints, each countersigned by three surviving members of the "Ten Horsepower" aircrew and the Tower Officer of the day.

Overall size 32¼x23½ inches
Image size 27½x17¾ inches
Price $125
Plus $5 shipping & handling

"Valor at Polebrook" may be ordered from:

RICK SCHOOL
P.O. Box 83
Kimberly, WI 54136
(920) 730-8212

SPOFFORD HOUSE

© 1993 Spofford House

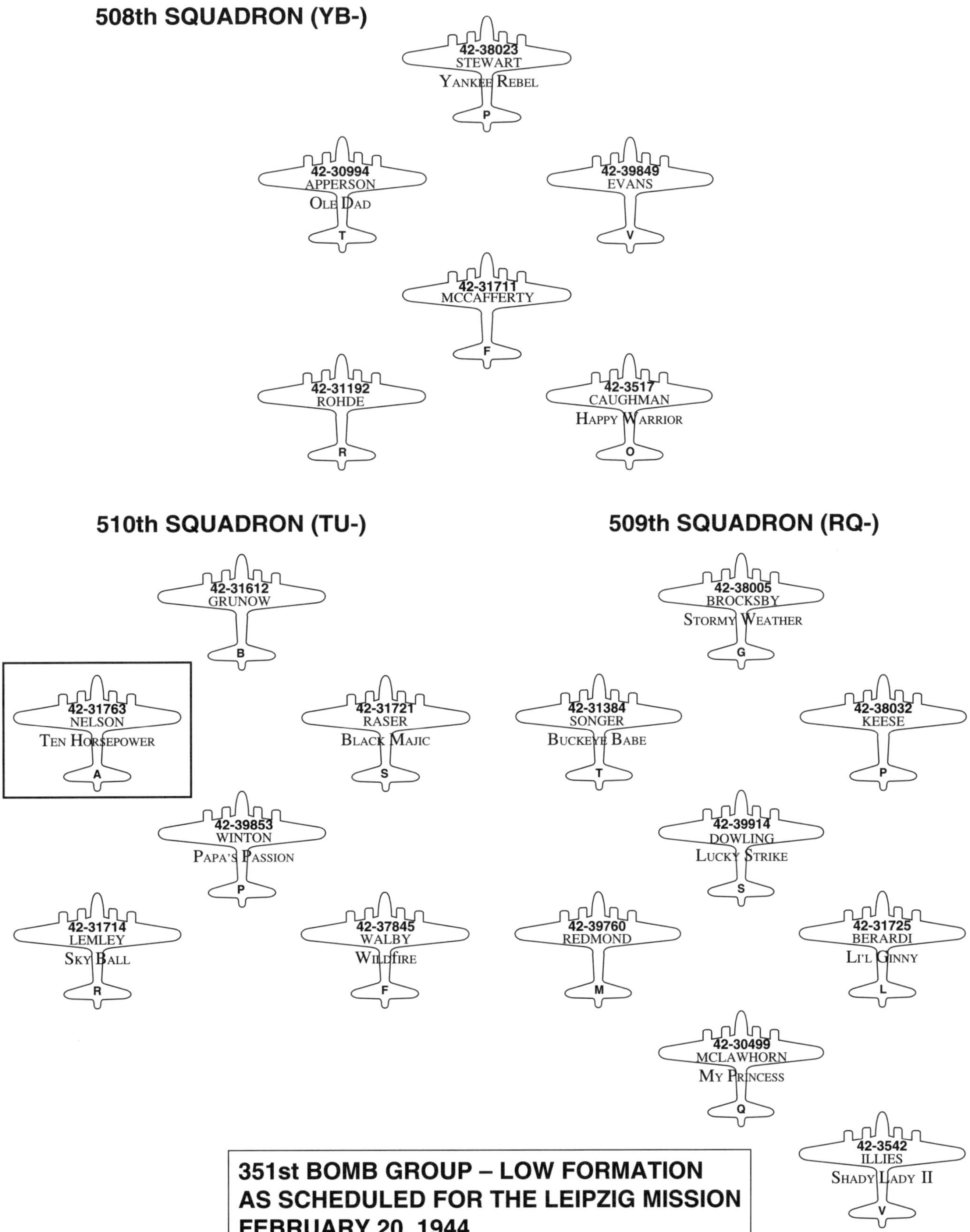

Mission 81

508th SQUADRON (YB-)

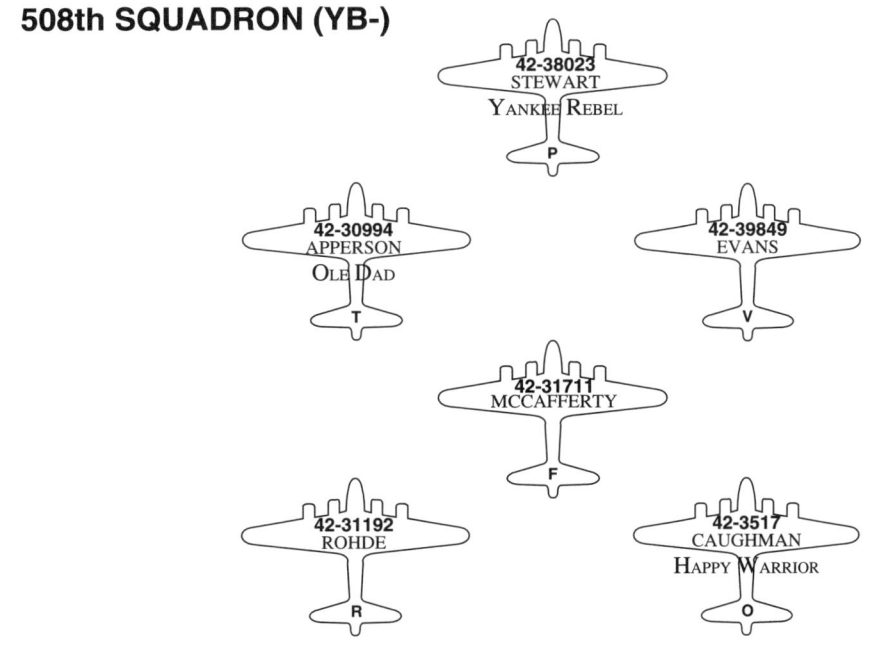

42-38023 STEWART — Yankee Rebel (P)
42-30994 APPERSON — Ole Dad (T)
42-39849 EVANS (V)
42-31711 MCCAFFERTY (F)
42-31192 ROHDE (R)
42-3517 CAUGHMAN — Happy Warrior (O)

510th SQUADRON (TU-)

42-31612 GRUNOW (B)
42-31763 NELSON — Ten Horsepower (A)
42-31721 RASER — Black Majic (S)
42-39853 WINTON — Papa's Passion (P)
42-31714 LEMLEY — Sky Ball (R)
42-37845 WALBY — Wildfire (F)

509th SQUADRON (RQ-)

42-38005 BROCKSBY — Stormy Weather (G)
42-31384 SONGER — Buckeye Babe (T)
42-38032 KEESE (P)
42-39914 DOWLING — Lucky Strike (S)
42-39760 REDMOND (M)
42-31725 BERARDI — Li'l Ginny (L)
42-30499 MCLAWHORN — My Princess (Q)
42-3542 ILLIES — Shady Lady II (V)

351st BOMB GROUP – LOW FORMATION AS SCHEDULED FOR THE LEIPZIG MISSION FEBRUARY 20, 1944

Valor at Polebrook

B-17 left the ground. By 0925 the last aircraft of the Leipzig group was airborne. This plane, 42-30499, was a flying spare from the 509th squadron. '499 was coded RQ-Q, and carried the name My Princess on its nose. This plane would fill the gap left in the formation if one of the bombers developed mechanical trouble over the English Channel. If not needed, it would return to Polebrook.

While the other planes were taking off, ground personnel worked frantically to pull Ten Horsepower from the mud. Tense moments passed as tow tractors and planks wrestled against the weight of fuel, ammunition and bombs. The machines finally won, but by the time the big right tire rolled on solid ground again the main runway was in constant use by planes being launched for the Oschersleben strike. Nelson had to wait until the last aircraft was away before moving into position and pushing the throttles forward. Ten Horsepower lifted off from the east-west runway at 0940. By that time, the rest of the group was already above the clouds and forming up over Deenethorpe.

Nelson knew that by flying directly to intercept the group enroute to the target he could shorten the distance to make up for lost time. His first task, however, was to get his own bomber through the clouds and on its way up to twenty thousand feet, the assigned cruising altitude for the mission. He expected to find the formation somewhere along the way. Ten Horsepower weighed nearly sixty thousand pounds at take-off. According to the B-17 pilot's manual, the best rate of climb the heavy plane could achieve was only six hundred feet per minute. Nelson knew this was based on standard procedures for a normal situation, and that if he was careful he could do better. On Nelson's command, Flight Officer Bartley retracted the landing gear and raised the flaps. Nelson throttled back somewhat, moved the prop pitch levers until the tachometers showed twenty-five hundred RPMs, then adjusted the superchargers for forty-six inches of manifold pressure. This power setting gave him a climb rate of just over seven hundred feet per minute and an airspeed of one hundred fifty miles per hour. Nelson knew that his climb rate would drop off as he gained altitude, and that he'd have to steadily advance the throttles to keep the engines developing full power. Above ten thousand feet, he'd frequently readjust the superchargers to maintain manifold pressure. Nelson and Bartley were always busy while in the cockpit. The airplane required their constant attention.

With airspeed and climb established, Lt. Nelson rolled the elevator trim wheel to ease the resistance he felt through the control column. Without elevator trim, Nelson would have quickly become fatigued by having to continuously pull against the wheel to maintain the climb. Flight Officer Bartley adjusted the cowl flaps for optimum engine cooling, visually checked the two engines on his side of the plane, and keyed his intercom mic (microphone) to report "Everything A-O-K" to his skipper. The intercom was essential to communication in the cockpit, and throughout the plane. One would quickly become hoarse trying to shout above the continuous thunder of the engines, and would not be clearly heard if he tried. The headphones did not block the engine noise, but they did put the amplified voices directly into the listeners' ears. A crew would have a serious problem if the intercom was knocked out at a crucial time in battle.

Ten Horsepower seemed to crawl as it climbed toward the overcast. Nelson occasionally glanced to his left to check engines one and two but his primary task was to watch the flight instruments, keep the wings level and the airspeed constant. The windshields went gray and water-streaked as the plane entered the thick blanket of clouds. Depth perception was lost in the fog. Every man strained to catch a glimpse of other airplanes in time to avoid crashing into them. Nelson was now unable to see the ground for an attitude reference and was totally dependent on his instruments. He constantly cross-checked airspeed and rate of climb to maintain a steady ascent while using the gyro-horizon to keep the wings level. To keep Ten Horsepower under control in the clouds required Nelson's complete concentration. It took less than five minutes for '763 to break out above the clouds. To the ten airmen on board, they were five very long minutes.

At eight thousand feet, to prevent the superchargers from over-speeding, Lt. Nelson called for Flight Officer Bartley to turn off the carburetor air filters. At ten thousand feet, Nelson advised the crew to put on their oxygen masks. He checked airspeed and climb rate for the hundredth time and continued to look for other aircraft in the area around him. In clear skies and with good visibility, Ten Horsepower flew east toward the English Channel.

The climb to altitude was always a drawn out process for so heavily loaded an aircraft. Lagging behind as they were, progress seemed pathetically slow to Nelson and Bartley. Even with the weight reduction from the fuel burn, vertical speed decreased as they gained altitude. Thirty minutes after takeoff, Ten Horsepower was nearing the twelve thousand foot mark. The climb rate was now only five hundred feet per minute. From his navigator's station forward of and below the cockpit, Lt. Truemper reported that they were properly on the intercept course he had computed. Lt. Martin leaned into the Plexiglas nose bubble and searched the distant sky for some sign of the formation. Ten Horsepower carried no bombsight that day. Martin would have to release his bombs when he saw bombs falling from the lead plane, as would the rest of the group. Until they reached the target, Joe Martin would be a gunner and observer. At present he had nothing to report. Martin scanned the cloud-horizon, and waited.

Shortly before 1100, Lt. Martin sighted the 351st group as it was climbing through fifteen thousand feet. Ron Bartley verified the group's "Triangle J" markings, and Nelson steered to join the formation. It was important to move into position as quickly as possible, to gain the protection of the group's massed firepower. Due to the direct route calculated by Lt. Truemper, and the maximum climb rate Lt. Nelson had maintained, Ten Horsepower was several hundred feet higher than the rest of the group. Nelson leveled off temporarily, while the formation continued its climb. The lone bomber gradually converged with the nineteen other Fortresses, and Nelson maneuvered to get into position. Strict radio silence had to be maintained. Apart from a few crewmen waving from the windows of nearby aircraft, no greetings could be exchanged. Nelson formed up on the left wing of the lead aircraft in the low box, then reset throttles and props to match the climb rate of the group. The men of Ten Horsepower had overcome their first obstacle. More would be encountered before the day was over.

Valor at Polebrook

508th SQUADRON (YB-)

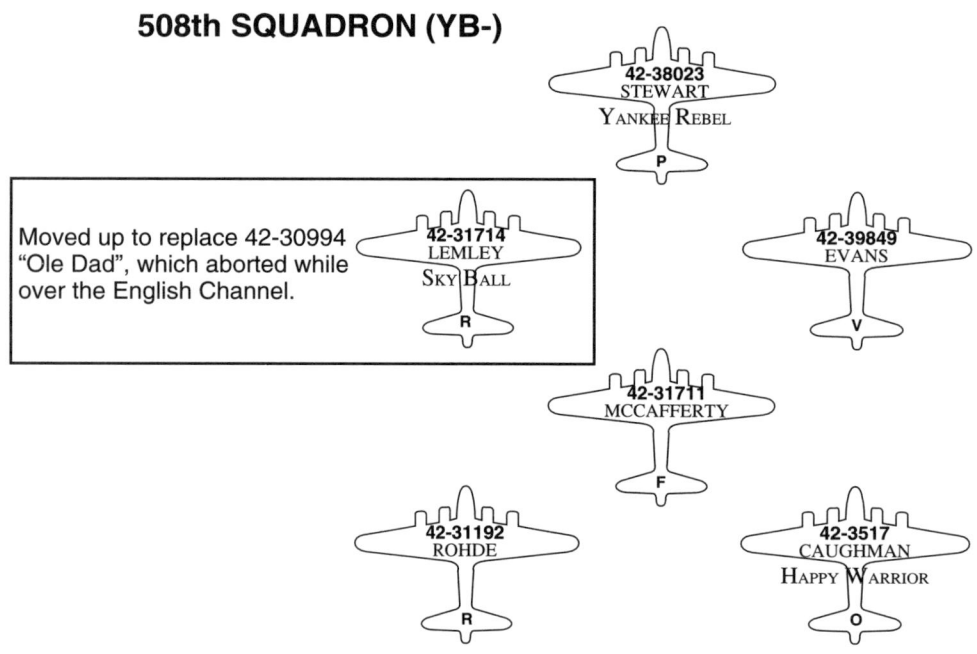

- 42-38023 STEWART — Yankee Rebel — P
- 42-31714 LEMLEY — Sky Ball — R *(Moved up to replace 42-30994 "Ole Dad", which aborted while over the English Channel.)*
- 42-39849 EVANS — V
- 42-31711 MCCAFFERTY — F
- 42-31192 ROHDE — R
- 42-3517 CAUGHMAN — Happy Warrior — O

510th SQUADRON (TU-)

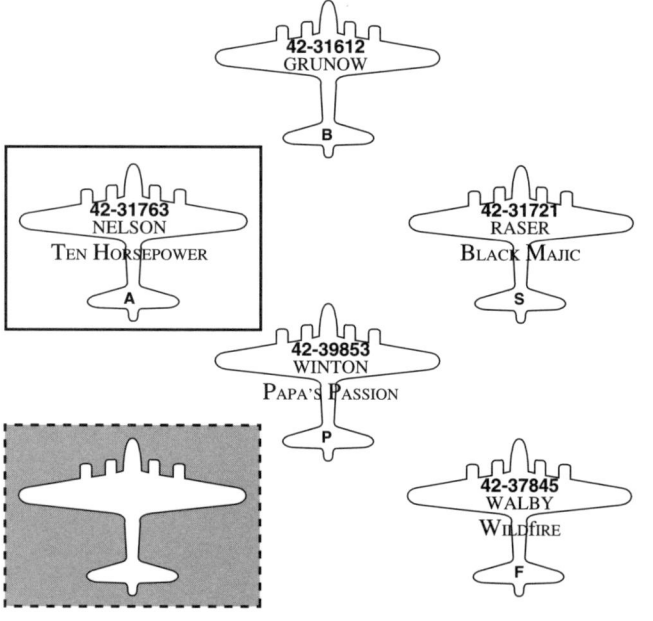

- 42-31612 GRUNOW — B
- 42-31763 NELSON — Ten Horsepower — A
- 42-31721 RASER — Black Majic — S
- 42-39853 WINTON — Papa's Passion — P
- 42-37845 WALBY — Wildfire — F

351st BOMB GROUP – LOW FORMATION ON APPROACH TO THE INITIAL POINT NORTHEAST OF LEIPZIG FEBRUARY 20, 1944

POSITIONS OPENED BY AIRCRAFT MOVEMENTS

509th SQUADRON (RQ-)

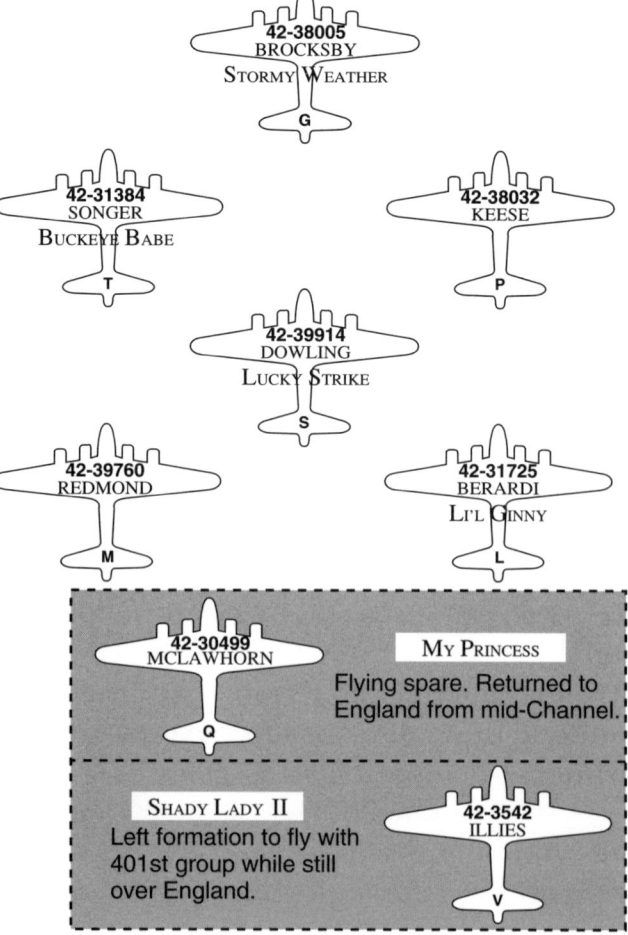

- 42-38005 BROCKSBY — Stormy Weather — G
- 42-31384 SONGER — Buckeye Babe — T
- 42-38032 KEESE — P
- 42-39914 DOWLING — Lucky Strike — S
- 42-39760 REDMOND — M
- 42-31725 BERARDI — Li'l Ginny — L
- 42-30499 MCLAWHORN — Q — **My Princess** — Flying spare. Returned to England from mid-Channel.
- **Shady Lady II** — Left formation to fly with 401st group while still over England.
- 42-3542 ILLIES — V

40

Mission 81

It took nearly thirty more minutes for the group to finish the climb. By the time Lt. Nelson's altimeter showed twenty thousand feet, there had been some changes in the formation. In mid-Channel, Ole Dad (42-30994, flown by Lt. Apperson) developed engine trouble and pulled out of the lead box to return to base. Shady Lady II, (42-3542, Lt. Illies) one of the group's flying spare aircraft, had been dispatched to another formation. The other spare, My Princess (42-30499, Lt. McLawhorn) had left the group to return to Polebrook. Sky Ball (42-31714, Lt. Lemley) moved forward from the low box to fill the gap opened by Ole Dad. This left the 510th squadron's box with only five aircraft.

Lt. Nelson leveled off at twenty thousand feet and worked to hold his position in the formation. Flight Officer Bartley set the engine controls for cruise flight. By adjusting the props for 2100 rpm and reducing turbo-boost to 31 inches, Bartley coaxed the airspeed needle up to 157 mph. The thirsty engines had gulped 400 gallons of fuel during the climb to altitude. Knowing that each engine would swallow another fifty gallons per hour, Nelson moved the mixture levers to the Auto Lean position for maximum range. He scanned the instrument panel again, then called for the crew to test their guns and check in. The plane shook with the recoil as each gunner fired a few short bursts into the empty air around them. One by one, the men reported that they were ready for combat. Nelson reminded the crew to keep a sharp watch for enemy fighters. There was no magic line to cross before they would be attacked. The Luftwaffe could come at any time.

The Luftwaffe was ready. It did not take long for German fighters to find the group as it droned steadily eastward. At 1125, aircraft 42-31711 (Lt. McCafferty), flying deputy lead position in the 508th squadron, was attacked head on by an Me109. Five minutes later, as the group crossed the coast of Holland, another Messerschmitt rolled in at '711 from dead ahead with cannons firing. At 1200, and now over Germany, '711 was singled out for a firing run by a third Me109. None of these attacks caused any damage, and each was met with fierce defensive fire. At 1205, an Me109 was shot down by the right waist gunner of 42-31612 (Lt. Grunow), the lead plane of the 510th squadron. A FW 190 was shot down by the left waist gunner of Black Majic (42-31712, Lt. Raser) at the same time. At 1245, southeast of Hanover, an Me109 struck at Buckeye Babe (42-31384, Lt. Songer) of the 509th squadron while another 509th ship, Lucky Strike (42-39914, Lt. Dowling), was attacked from behind. Tail attacks were not unheard of, but the Luftwaffe's usual tactic was to approach the bombers from head on, as the closing speed of the planes made for a swift attack and left little time for gunners to shoot back. The chin turret carried by the B-17G was specifically designed as protection against these devastating frontal attacks.

During the thirty-nine minutes between Hanover and Wittenberg, individual fighters made attacks against the bombers at nearly regular intervals. The attacks intensified as the group flew nearer to the target. Yankee Rebel was again leading the formation, with Sgt. Bartholomew Hagan firing back at the German fighters. Hagan's February 20th diary passage describes extremes of heat and cold: *"Today was our farthest penetration into Germany. We were group lead with Lt. Floden as pilot and Major Stewart as commander. We took off at 9:10,*

Valor at Polebrook

A Messerschmitt Me109 similar to those that struck Ten Horsepower. (National Air and Space Museum, Smithsonian Institution. Photo No. 33192)

made a good assembly and took off across the channel, climbing all the way. We were going in at 20,000 feet. The temp was -30°. We hit some light flak over the enemy coast. Pretty inaccurate. About 20 minutes from the IP we were jumped by about 30 Me109s and Fw190s. They came in at 12 O'clock and barrel rolled right through the formation. P-47s came in at 3 O'clock and there was a hell of a dogfight with (Messerschmitts) hitting the deck. Flak was heavy and accurate over the target! Got a few flak holes in our right wing. No fighters or flak on the way home. Blew the target sky high."

Despite the intensity of the attacks, 351st gunners shot down three fighters and damaged a fourth. The victories, however, were not entirely one-sided. The formation began the turn onto the bomb run at the Initial Point, twenty miles northeast of Leipzig, at 1334. By this time, Nelson and crew were no longer with them.

The exact minute cannot be pinpointed, but sometime during the massed attack described by Sgt. Hagan two Me109s swooped down from high and to the right and fired on Ten Horsepower. Twenty millimeter cannon shells shattered the copilot's overhead window and exploded in the cockpit. Flight Officer Bartley was instantly decapitated. Shell fragments ricocheted through the cockpit and pelted the right side of Lt. Nelson's face with such force that Nelson was knocked unconscious. The stricken pilots slumped forward across the control columns, and the plane began to lose altitude.

Joe Martin saw the Messerschmitts begin their diving attack. He gave a warning over the intercom and was firing back at them when he felt their cannon shells exploding against the bomber. Martin's realization that the cockpit had been hit and the sensation of the nose pitching downward occurred simultaneously. His first reaction was to scramble aft and stand up through the opening in the floor between the pilot's seats. Martin's stomach tightened in horror at the carnage on the flight deck. Convinced that both pilots were dead, a terrified Martin crab-walked back to his bombardier station and called over the intercom for the crew to abandon ship. He then threw the switches that would open the bomb bay doors and release the bomb load, to give the others a clear way out.

Mission 81

As Joe Martin fired back with the chin turret, Carl Moore swung around to bring his top turret guns in line with the Messerschmitts. The attack was over in seconds. (Photo by Jeff Rogers)

Certain that the plane was doomed, Martin staggered back below the cockpit, opened the escape hatch in the belly, and bailed out.

Now the entire 510th box was being attacked by fighters. Crewmen on other bombers were busy defending their own planes, and had only seconds to see what happened as Ten Horsepower began to go down. In Papa's Passion (42-39853, Lt. Winton), Sgt. Ted Woodhave saw the attack on Nelson's plane: "I was in the left waist position of our plane, and the Nelson crew was off to our left, ahead and a little higher than us. I watched the 20 millimeter shells exploding like snowballs being thrown against the side of the plane, then the direct hit. One crewman jumped out of the nose just after impact of the shell. The plane went into a shallow dive. I can't describe it as a spin, but there were quite a few enemy planes attacking, and I lost eye contact with the Nelson plane."

In Black Majic, radio-gunner Elmer Ruschman watched what he thought would be the end of the crew he had flown with only two days earlier: "We were flying just off of Nelson's right wing. When Nelson's plane was hit, they dropped their bombs in seconds. The loss of the bomb weight gave them a little upward movement, taking them above and behind us, off to our left. A man came out the front escape hatch almost immediately after the bombs dropped, and the plane nosed down into a dive. The view from my position was not good after that. When a plane takes a dive, it disappears in a hurry. I never saw them after they fell out of formation. I didn't expect any of them to survive."

Valor at Polebrook

With the two pilots pressing against the controls, Ten Horsepower slipped into a spiraling right turn which gradually tightened as the diving plane built up speed. Centrifugal force pulled heavily against the crewmen standing at their guns. All soon realized that the plane was out of control, but none of the men had time to see what was happening to the others on board. Although they were relatively close together in the fuselage, each man remembers the immediate confusion from his own perspective.

In the radio room, Joe Rex tried to comprehend what was happening: "I knew we were hit. Lt. Nelson rang the bail-out bell. I was going to jump, but the plane went into a spin. I couldn't move. I tried to hang onto my gun, but I was pulled down to the floor."

At the left waist gun position, Tom Sowell was also powerless against the force of the spiral: "The first thing I knew was that fighters were coming in. Someone on the crew called it out, but I'm not sure who it was. The next thing I remember is the ringing of the (bail out) bell, and that my parachute was missing. I wasn't wearing it, and when we went into the spin, my chute hit the door of the radio room where Joe Rex was. I was pressed down against the floor. I couldn't lift a finger to save myself.

At the right waist gun, Russell Robinson didn't have a chance to fire at the Messerschmitts: "When the first attack came in I saw one of those planes flash by the right wing in a steep dive. Then it was gone. I heard the explosion in the cockpit, and almost immediately our plane nosed down and went into a spin. For the next few minutes it was like being inside of a spinning top. We were thrown against the side of the fuselage and held there. We couldn't move."

Russell Robinson beneath the right waist gun of a B-17.

Up in the top turret, Carl Moore had a clear view of the attacking German fighters: *"I was just swinging around in my turret toward the front when two Messerschmitt 109s came at us almost head on. I could see their cannons firing as they came in. They flashed by on the right and at the same time there was an explosion in the cockpit. We peeled away to the right and at first I thought we were taking ordinary evasive action. When we first left the formation it was a smooth pull-away, but it got tighter and tighter until no one could stand up."*

It may seem like a minor point that Rex, Sowell and Robinson describe their spiraling aircraft as being in a "spin", but there was nothing minor about the danger they were in. All sense of time was lost as the trapped men struggled in vain to save themselves. The roar of the engines was driven from their ears by the pressure on their heads. The three alarm bells rang continuously, adding their urgent call to the din, but the intercom remained ominously silent. No one could lift a hand to key their mic button.

Carl Moore was nearly slung to the floor below his turret but he managed to muscle his way forward into the cockpit and stand up behind the pilots' seats. The sub-zero hurricane shrieking in through the smashed overhead window lashed at the gunner and drove him backwards. Moore squinted against the wind, leaned forward to see past the armor plating, and recoiled in horror. To Moore's right, Ron Bartley's lifeless body had folded forward across his seat belt and onto the yoke, a ghastly wound where his head should have been. To Moore's left, Lt. Nelson was also slumped forward, unconscious and bleeding from the wounds in his face. Moore was stunned. The gruesome scene was something he had never expected, and was too much to comprehend all at once.

Amidst this chaos, Carl Moore fought to keep a grip on his senses. *He* had to get the falling plane under control. With the death of all on board a certainty if he failed, his survival instinct took over. Fear would not leave, but panic was swept away by adrenaline as Carl tried to reach the control wheels. There was no floor directly between the pilots' seats, as this space was the entrance to the crawl-way going forward into the nose. Moore straddled the hole, and wedged his bulky flight boots between the rails of the seat support structures. With this precarious footing established, he leaned over the center pedestal and grabbed each control wheel with one hand. Moore had to force his elbows against the pilots' chests to push them back off of the controls. His hunched-over position was incredibly awkward. It was nearly impossible for him to keep his balance and hold the pilots out of his way. The plane was still gaining speed, which tightened the spiral and put more force on the men inside. Moore managed to pull the throttles back, but he had no time to check rpm or to change prop settings. The clouds and ground whirled crazily outside the windshield, and Moore had no means of telling which way was "up". It seemed that everything was working against him as he fought to stay alive. He held on to the control wheels and prayed for all he was worth.

After a descent of more than five thousand feet, Carl Moore managed to get the wings level. Then he began to pull out of the dive. As the plane zoomed back into controlled flight, the force on the crew increased even more. Russell Robinson says that where the spiral flattened the men, the pull-out crushed them. He compares the feeling to being on a carnival ride that "spins and plasters you up against the wall with the G-forces." Tom Sowell's recollection of the pull-out is more succinct: "I felt like my eyeballs were going to pop out through my cheek bones."

Ten Horsepower was again in level flight but was not really back under control. Sgt. Moore could not relax, as the pilots' bodies still rested against his elbows, nor could he let go of the yokes, as the plane would fall out of control again. Moore's intercom was useless. His mic and head-set wires had been pulled from their control panel when he moved forward into the cockpit. Even if they had still been plugged in, he had no free hand with which to key his mic. As the seconds went by, Sgt. Moore began to look around the cockpit. He glanced down between his feet, and noticed that the forward escape hatch was open.

Valor at Polebrook

Carl Moore stands near his workplace. Note the window above the copilot's seat. With this window shot away, the cockpit structure formed a scoop that deflected the slipstream directly into the face of the man in the seat.

Then he turned to look behind himself and saw that the bomb bay doors were open, and that the bombs were gone. A torrent of frozen air rushed through the cockpit and out the bomb bay. For the first time since the fighters attacked, Moore realized that he was shivering.

It had been bitterly cold inside the aircraft before the attack. Now, with some cockpit windows shot out, the sub-zero temperature was dangerously intensified by the blast of the slipstream. Since leveling off, the icy roar had subsided only slightly, but it was enough to let the shaken gunner realize that the alarm bells were still ringing, and would keep ringing until someone turned them off. The alarm switch was on a panel on Lt. Nelson's side of the cockpit. Moore leaned across the unconscious pilot to look for the switch, but as soon as he took his hand off of the control wheel the plane's nose lifted and airspeed began to drop off. Moore grabbed the wheel and pushed forward to level off again. He reached for the switch a second time, and again the bomber gained altitude. Moore did get the bells turned off, but in the process he had discovered that unless constant forward pressure was maintained on the control wheels, the plane would begin to climb. With tired arms and aching legs, Moore leaned against the controls and

Mission 81

waited for someone to come up and help him.

When Lt. Truemper could move again after the bomber leveled off, he crawled to the cockpit to see what was going on. His first view as he emerged from the crawl-way was of Carl Moore's backside as the young gunner struggled to keep the plane level. Moore later reported, *"When Lt. Truemper came up, I asked what course to take. He told me to take a heading of 300 degrees. I kept hold of the controls until I got the compass on 300 and then handed the ship over to him. I went back and closed the bomb bay doors and then returned to the cockpit. Some of the control cables had been shot away and the ship was hard to manage."*

Freed from the force of the spiral, the dazed crewmen in the aft fuselage began to recover from the attack. Tom Sowell found his parachute and buckled it on. His adrenaline surged again as the plane climbed and dove while Moore was trying to turn off the alarm bells. The motion confused Sowell but he kept his wits about him. The lanky Texan helped Archie Mathies climb out of the ball turret, then returned to his waist gun.

As soon as he was out of the ball, Sgt. Mathies started forward to find out what was happening in the cockpit. He had to pass through the radio room to get there. Joe Rex remembers that *he* was just preparing to leave: "After Carl pulled the plane out, I was going to bail out through the bomb bay. Archie grabbed me by the shoulder and pointed over to the corner of the compartment, to where my parachute was. I didn't wear my 'chute when we were flying, because it was impossible to fit it under my flak vest. In the confusion, I'd forgotten to put it on. I almost jumped without it."

In the cockpit, Walter Truemper tried to get a feel for the damaged plane. Just as Carl Moore had done, Truemper stood between the seats and braced his elbows against the bodies of the pilots to keep them from interfering with the controls. Soon Carl Moore returned from closing the bomb bay doors. Archie Mathies was right behind him, but did not yet know what had happened. The howl of the slipstream was deafening. Mathies had to shout to be heard. Sgt. Moore wordlessly pointed to the dead and wounded pilots. Lt. Truemper turned sideways to yell over his shoulder, and informed the two sergeants that the bombardier had bailed out. Truemper asked about the rest of the crew. Mathies reported the waist gunners and radioman still on board. Archie's first concern was for the pilots. It appeared that little could be done to help Lt. Nelson. Flight Officer Bartley was obviously dead.

Amidst the roar of the engines and the freezing air rushing through the cockpit, Mathies, Moore, and Truemper had to overcome the shock of seeing their stricken crewmates and quickly assess how badly Ten Horsepower had been damaged. As the only conscious officer remaining on board, Lt. Walter Truemper was in command. With the two engineers he determined that, apart from the damage to the cockpit and some control cables, the plane was still airworthy. All four engines were running, and there did not appear to be any fuel leaks. It seemed likely that the plane would be capable of making the flight home, but none of them really knew how to fly. The short lessons that Lt. Nelson had given them were never intended for a long distance, cross country flight over enemy territory. It seemed wrong to Truemper to abandon a flyable aircraft. Even so, he gave the crew the option of bailing out. While the

Valor at Polebrook

gunners talked, the navigator-in-command mentally plotted the route back. After only a brief discussion, the men reported their desire to remain with the plane as long as possible before jumping, and to hopefully make it back to England. The crew's response only confirmed the decision that Lt. Truemper had already made.

Truemper's next decision was to begin a descent to get the airplane below ten thousand feet, where the crew would not need their oxygen masks. The air temperature would still be below the freezing mark, but any additional warmth would help. Truemper's other thought was to get closer to the clouds, where they might find concealment if more fighters showed up. He reminded the men to keep their guns moving, as German pilots were trained to look for gun positions that appeared unmanned.

Walter Truemper's mind raced as the impact of what was happening began to take hold on him. After a few more minutes in the cockpit he handed the controls over to Sgt. Mathies, then climbed down into the crawlway to return to his chart table. On the map before him, Truemper circled what he calculated as the position where they were first attacked. He then drew a straight line connecting that point to Polebrook. Ten Horsepower was heading for home.

The remaining 351st aircraft continued to the target without Ten Horsepower.

Chapter Four: Back to England

For Joe Rex, the decision to return to England marked the beginning of an ordeal that would be concluded during the next five hours, but would linger for the next fifty years. After Sgt. Mathies left the radio room to continue moving forward, Rex clipped on his parachute and stood to man his gun. Rex reports that within minutes, his services as a technician were required: "Not knowing exactly where we were after falling out of formation, Lt. Truemper gave Archie a tentative course, then tried to call me on the intercom but got nothing. (At this point, Carl Moore took over at the controls, freeing Archie Mathies to assist the radio operator.) On his way to the cockpit, Archie had seen where cannon shells had caused damage in the bomb bay. He showed me the wire routing through the bomb bay, so I could search for the break in the line. I found that a four inch section of wire had been shot out. I had a similar size wire in my tool kit, and I used this to fix the break. This restored communications between the radio compartment and the front of the ship."

While Joe Rex repaired the intercom wire in the bomb bay, Truemper, Mathies, and Moore struggled to move Ron Bartley's body from the right seat. It was a gruesome job, but a necessary one if the plane was to be flown back to England. With one man straddling the hatch and holding the control columns, the other two tried to lift the copilot out of his seat to lower him through the hatch and into the crawlway below the cockpit. In the cramped conditions, the job was nearly impossible. The automatic pilot was turned on to let the man between the seats get out of the way, but the plane immediately went into a dive. The autopilot was quickly turned off. The men fought against the copilot's inert weight, but could not move him. In sheer desperation they called Sgt. Rex to come forward from the bomb bay to help. While performing the hideous task, Rex did not realize that his flight suit was being smeared with the dead copilot's blood, which quickly froze into the leather. After an agonizing exertion, the copilot's body was secured in the crawlway. Rex returned to the radio room, horrified by what he had seen and done.

While the men in the cockpit wrestled against the weight of the copilot's body, Russell Robinson was alarmed to see that Ten Horsepower was not alone in the German sky: "With all this going on, Sowell and I kept watching for enemy fighters. I looked out my window and there were two FW 190s off our right wing. I couldn't believe what I was seeing, and I had to look

Valor at Polebrook

twice to be sure they weren't ours. I swung my gun on them and fired a few rounds, which caused them to back off some distance. They were just out of range of our fifty cal guns, but they were armed with 20mm cannon and were still in range to cause us some damage. They just flew alongside us for a while, then they made a pass at us."

The fighters swept inward toward the rear of the B-17, firing as they turned. Cannon shells raked across the right wing, and damaged the aileron. Other shells hit in the fuselage. Robinson continues: "One shell hit back toward the tail, around the strut of the tail wheel. Tom and I talked about it being awful close to Hagbo, but we couldn't go back to check on him. One shell went right between me and Tom. A hole opened up just over my head. We never could find where it went out. None of these were explosive type shells. If they had been, there would have been more casualties."

Even as the Focke-Wulfs were turning away after hitting the wing, another was diving on Ten Horsepower from above. With the men up front busy flying the plane, Joe Rex was the only gunner able to shoot back at the fighter. He opened up with the single machine gun mounted in the egg-shaped window above the radio room. At that same instant, the German fighter began firing twenty-millimeter rounds at the B-17. Cannon shells tore through the Plexiglas, showering the young radio operator with metal fragments. Rex was painfully wounded in the right hand and arm, but his bullets had found their mark. The Focke-Wulf exploded, sending debris hurtling past the bomber.

Top view of a B-17 in flight. This would have been the last thing seen by the pilot of the FW190 shot down by Joe Rex.

Stunned and bleeding, Joe Rex collapsed to the floor. At first, his shipmates didn't realize he had been hit. When Joe didn't answer on the intercom, Carl Moore and Tom Sowell went to the radio room and found him lying among the spent shell casings from his machine gun. The two gunners gave Rex some morphine from the first aid kit, and bandaged his wounds. When the pain killer took effect, Rex felt strong enough to resume his duties. The cannon shells that wounded Rex also hit some of his radio gear. In spite of his injuries, the young technician began to diagnose the damage and determine which systems were still functioning. Moore and Sowell told Rex to call them if he had trouble, then returned to their gun stations.

Back to England

A Focke-Wulf 190, the type of fighter that wounded Joe Rex and damaged Ten Horsepower's right wing. (National Air and Space Museum, Smithsonian Institution. Photo No. 46002)

These waist gunners on a B-17F show how little space Sowell and Robinson had to work in. The shell that passed between them missed them purely by luck. (The Boeing Company Archives)

Valor at Polebrook

Looking aft through the radio room. From this position, Joe Rex shot down the Focke Wulf 190 that wounded him. (The Boeing Company Archives)

Sgt. Joe Rex, upon completion of flexible gunnery training.

In Ten Horsepower's shattered cockpit, it did not take long for Mathies, Moore, and Truemper to see that none of them would be able to fly the crippled bomber the entire way back to England. The freezing winds blasting through the empty window frame stabbed at their bodies and numbed their minds. No one could withstand the cold and pain for more than a few minutes at a time. The three novice pilots set up a rotation of flying, manning the top turret, and trying to warm up again. Each time they switched positions, the man in the copilot's seat had to climb out first and lean across Lt. Nelson to hold his control wheel while the next man climbed past the pedestal and into the copilot's seat. It was an awkward transition which required some strenuous contortions from the men in their bulky flightsuits. Every ten to fifteen minutes, the plane bucked and dove while the men in the cockpit climbed around each other. It was easier to fly from the copilot's seat, but after only a few minutes at the controls each man's hands and face went numb from the penetrating cold.

Sgt. Moore soon realized that their survival might depend on being able to fly from the left seat, away from the shot-out windows. At one point, when Lt. Truemper had gone forward into the nose and Archie Mathies was flying, Moore decided to try to move Lt. Nelson but could not do it alone. Russell Robinson was coming forward to see what was happening in the cockpit. He arrived just in time to help: "Lt. Nelson was sitting in his seat, not moving. His face was pock-marked, with many little bloody spots where the shell fragments had hit him. They wanted to move Nelson, so they could fly from his seat, out of the wind. There wasn't a lot of room. The prop controls and throttles were right there, and we bumped

Back to England

them. The plane was already hard to control, and that just made it worse."

While trying to move Lt. Nelson, Robinson and Moore became certain that he was still alive. Fearing that further attempts to move their pilot would only aggravate his injuries, it was decided that Nelson would be left in his seat. With nothing else to do in the cockpit, Robinson returned to his waist gun to continue looking for enemy fighters. Sgt. Moore moved back into his turret. Lt. Truemper relieved Sgt. Mathies at the controls.

Walter Truemper was known for his calmness in tense situations, but in the copilot's seat, the wind beating at his face, his friend dying in the seat next to him, and seven men under his command, the navigator-turned-pilot felt a fear and uncertainty like none he had ever faced. As he always had throughout his life, Walter prayed to God for guidance and strength, and added a word for the lives of his fellow crewmen.

Inexperienced though they were, Truemper, Mathies and Moore had managed to keep Ten Horsepower at a more or less constant altitude just above the cloud layer, but now the ground was becoming more frequently visible through breaks in the overcast. Inevitably, German gun crews spotted the bomber and fired at it. Flak began to burst overhead, too high to do any real damage, but the effect was unnerving. The gunners corrected their aim. Black puffs blossomed closer and closer to the lone B-17. Some of the exploding shells began to shake the plane. The biting smell of burnt gunpowder was drawn into the ship through the escape

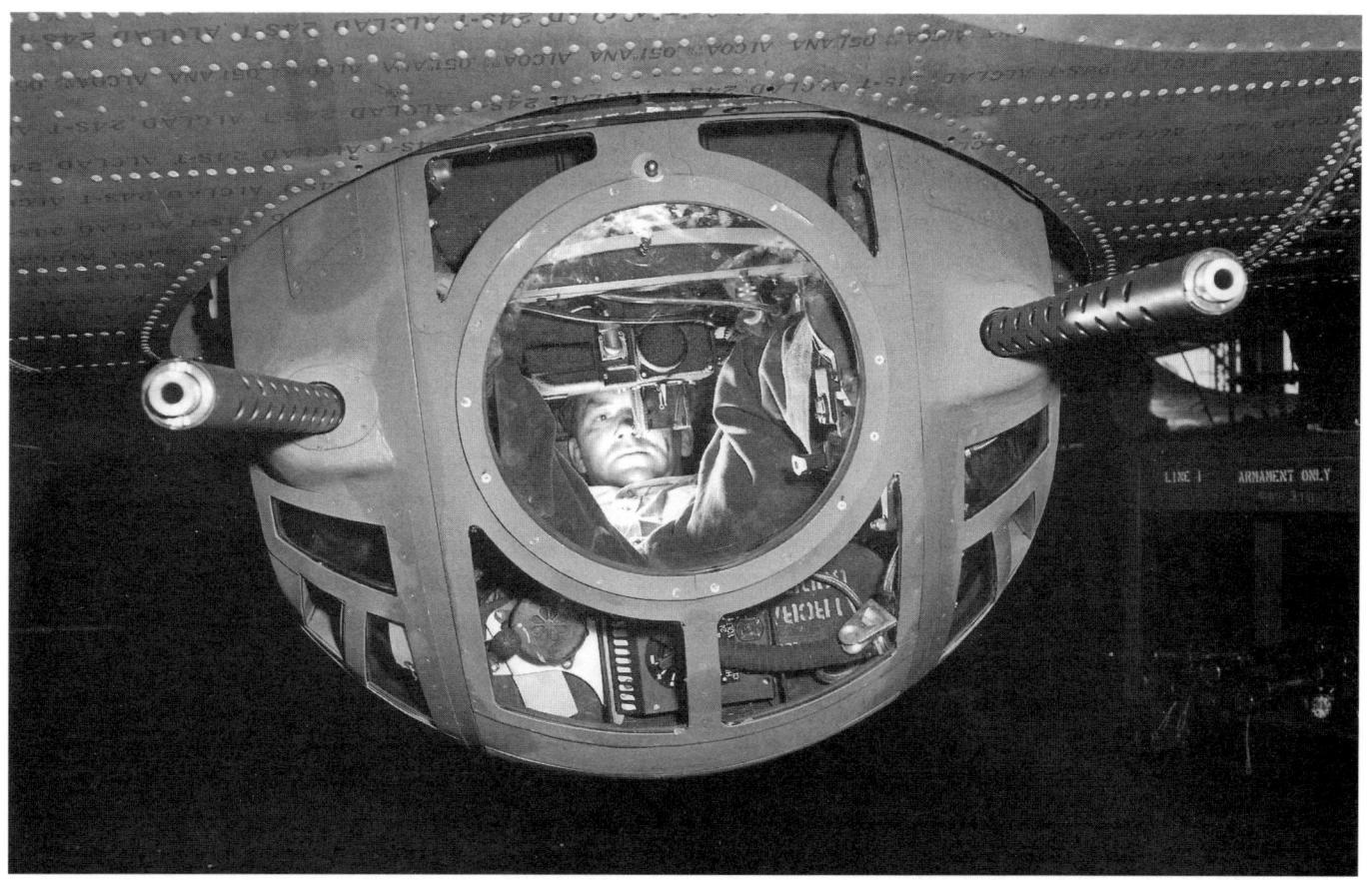

This photo illustrates the small size of the ball turret. Tom Sowell barely fit inside, but kept the guns moving in an effort to discourage further Luftwaffe attacks. (The Boeing Company Archives)

Valor at Polebrook

hatch, still open below the nose. Walter Truemper was already fighting the damaged controls. He could not take evasive action, nor did he know how. It was all he could do to keep the wings level and the altitude constant. Frightened, but not panicking, Lt. Truemper decided to steer into the clouds, to try to throw off the flak gunners' aim.

The flak stopped as quickly as it had begun. The fliers hoped the flak crews had lost sight of them when the bomber entered the clouds, but all knew that ground guns would sometimes stop firing to allow Luftwaffe fighters a clear path for attack. Truemper cautiously lifted Ten Horsepower out of the clouds, and waited to hear gunfire. At the left waist window, Tom Sowell scanned his section of the sky for the tiny black dots that would quickly grow into Messerschmitts or Focke-Wulfs. He was ready to fight back: "Lt. Truemper had told us all to get in the gun positions and keep the guns moving, because German fighters would see a gun not moving or rotating, and they'd attack that position. Archie was still up front, so after a while I crawled into his ball turret. I was too big. My feet just about covered up the sight. We were at about five thousand feet over Germany. Through breaks in the clouds I could see everything going on in the streets of the little towns below. I flew that turret 'till we got back to England.

To the great relief of the crew, the Luftwaffe was busy elsewhere. The flak gunners had either lost sight of Ten Horsepower or lost interest in it. Even so, the men stayed at their guns, ready to defend the plane should it be spotted again.

With the flak temporarily silent, and the plane flying unsteadily westward just above the cloud layer, Lt. Truemper turned the controls over to Carl Moore. Truemper crawled into the nose again to tune the radio compass and get a position fix. The open escape hatch was only inches from his boots as he moved between it and Flight Officer Bartley's inert body. The immediate nearness of death must have been an overwhelming distraction, but somehow Walter Truemper blocked it out and concentrated on navigation. There is no way to know what went through his mind as he leaned across his chart table, but when Walter Truemper was faced with many reasons to question himself and the decisions he had made, he kept his faith in God, and kept his mind on his job.

The radio fixes convinced Lt. Truemper that they had reached the Dutch coast, and would soon be over the English Channel. He moved forward to the bombardier's chair and looked down through the clear nose bubble. If some familiar feature could be spotted on the ground their position might become more certain, but the cloud cover made pilotage difficult. No landmarks could be seen. Truemper was distracted from his search by something moving out in front of the plane. He looked up to see that flak had begun bursting around them again. Walter Truemper had had enough. He decided it was time to descend through the clouds and start looking for land.

After Joe Rex's encounter with the Focke-Wulf, the men had steered for the clouds whenever they thought they had spotted an enemy fighter. Each excursion into the mist would last only a minute or two before the fliers would cautiously emerge to look for their supposed attackers, and each time the foe would be nowhere in sight. Now the descent would keep the inexperienced pilots blind until they came out beneath the cloud layer. Archie and Carl both considered the

Back to England

The bombardier's station in the nose of the B-17. The drive mechanism for the chin turret is visible beneath the seat. The edge of the navigator's table can be seen in the lower left corner. (The Boeing Company Archives)

possibility that they would crash into the sea before they flew clear of the clouds. Each knew this was a risk they had to take if they were to get home alive. Truemper climbed past Sgt. Moore and into the right seat. He pulled the throttles back slightly. Ten Horsepower sank into the greyness.

Instrument flight in a B-17 was a demanding task even for a qualified flier. The steady droning of the engines could easily lull an inattentive pilot into a false sense of security. Without constant attention to airspeed and attitude, a pilot could become disoriented and allow the plane to slip into a slow, spiraling descent. Many undamaged aircraft were flown into the ground in this manner. With their pilots both out of action, it was very unlikely that the unskilled airmen would bring Ten Horsepower out of the clouds under control. Inexperience wasn't the only thing working against their chances for a successful descent. Russell Robinson explains: "The first time I went forward, they were moving the copilot, and I didn't get all the way to the cockpit. The second time, I took a look around. I saw the opening in the windows, on the right side.

Valor at Polebrook

The cockpit of the B-17 was Spartan but functional despite the confining space. Here the control columns have been pulled back to reveal the instruments. Throttle and propeller controls are at center. (The Boeing Company Archives)

The oxygen bottles behind the copilot's seat hadn't been hit, but I could see instruments that were totally out. Luckily, the airspeed indicator was working. If you have no feel for an airplane in a climb or dive, the airspeed tells you exactly what you're doing, if you're level, going up or going down. And that was working."

With some instruments out of action (though we can not be certain which ones), the flight through the clouds would be even more difficult. Only one man could steer the plane through its descent, but Lt. Truemper wanted help in watching the gauges that were still functional. Sgt. Mathies leaned forward between the seats, adding his eyes to Truemper's as the two scanned the instrument panels for signs of trouble. The altimeter unwound slowly, like the second hand of a clock running backwards, but to the fog-blinded navigator it seemed as if time was standing still. He watched the airspeed indicator, pushing harder or relaxing slightly on the control column to keep the needle at 170 miles per hour. For what seemed like an eternity, the flier had been holding a constant forward pressure against the resisting control

Back to England

Russell Robinson in full flying gear. American aircrews wore electrically heated, insulated flying suits to protect against the sub-zero temperatures at altitude. Still, many suffered frostbite or died due to freezing of their oxygen masks.

wheel. Truemper's arms ached from the exertion and the cold, but he could not let up.

The engines continued their steady growling. Their reassuring but deafening thunder was matched in volume by the blast of the slipstream rushing in through the smashed windows. Archie Mathies called out the altitude every five hundred feet, counting backward from five thousand and hoping to see the ground before he reached zero. Walter Truemper strained to see something - anything - through the windshield but gave up and focused entirely on the instrument panel. "Twenty five hundred," Mathies yelled. Truemper could hardly hear him above the wind. Fatigue was catching up to Walter. He was in agony from the frozen lashing he was taking. The exposed areas of his face were wind-burned and frost-bitten. His hands were swollen inside his thin gloves. In spite of this torment, Truemper watched the flight instruments and tried to recall the simple skills his now unconscious pilot had taught him. He could almost hear Dick Nelson's encouraging voice coaching him through the clouds... *airspeed constant, wings level, steady rate of descent...* "Two thousand," Mathies called out.

The engine noise changed oddly for an instant, then resumed it's even droning. Truemper's eyes went wide with fear as he scrambled to decipher the engine readings. The needles hadn't moved. Walter fought away the panic that comes from confusion and found the fuel gauge on the panel in front of him. He rotated the selector switch through all six positions. The tanks didn't appear to be empty, but he had no idea how many gallons were left, or if the gauges were even working. Walter swallowed unconsciously, and prayed that whatever fuel was still in the tanks would be enough.

The engines roared on, pulling them through the greyness as the altimeter steadily unwound toward their collision with Earth. "Fifteen hundred feet!," Mathies called out, but before he had finished the plane punched through the bottom of the cloud layer and emerged into clear air. Grey-green water greeted the fliers, ready to accept them into the frigid depths should the motors cough and fail. The wave-tops stretched away from them in all directions. There was no sign of land, but they were out of the clouds and still flying. Walter Truemper looked up through the empty window frame. "Thank you," he said aloud. His words were swallowed by the wind.

Valor at Polebrook

B-17s of the 351st Bomb Group at work, somewhere over occupied Europe. Note the heavy cloud layer far below, and the black puffs from flak exploding somewhat closer. Ten Horsepower had to fly through both to return to England.

The crew felt a growing optimism now that they were below the clouds. They still did not know exactly where they were, but they had faith in their navigator. Each man was sure that Lt. Truemper would get them back to England. At that moment, the only thing Walter Truemper was sure of was that he was frozen and close to collapse. The stress of the descent had taken a heavy toll. He was ready to let someone else fly the plane. Sgt. Mathies was there, standing by to relieve the shivering Lieutenant. Truemper slid across the seat, reached for the pilot's control column, swung his leg around the pedestal, and moved as close to Lt. Nelson as he could to let Archie move into the copilot's seat: "I've got it, Wally!" Mathies yelled above the wind. Truemper let go of the pilot's wheel and nearly fell backwards from between the seats. He needed to rest, and to think somewhere away from the blast of cold air in the cockpit. He clambered forward into the nose and sat in his navigator's chair. In one motion, he folded his arms on the table and let his head drop heavily onto them.

Archie Mathies held the compass steady on the westerly course they had maintained for the last few hours. Mathies

Back to England

was impressed by how well Lt. Truemper had held the plane in a nearly constant descent, and kept it level in the clouds, but he had been worried by the brief change in engine noise. He turned on the carburetor air filters and set the intercooler controls to increase the carb air intake temperature. The last thing he needed at that moment was for the engines to be killed by ice in the carburetors. Since breaking out under the clouds, Archie had noticed that they were flying through scattered patches of sleet and rain. Carb ice was a real danger.

Archie sorted through the thoughts crowding his mind. His instinct was to push the throttles forward and squeeze as much power out of the engines as he could, but that might mean using up their fuel before they reached land. The chilled engineer did not have his pilot's knowledge of prop settings and manifold pressures for specific airspeeds, but he knew how the intake systems worked. Archie set the props for 2100 rpm and added ten for the manifold pressure setting. All of the engine gauges were on the copilot's side of the instrument panel, which made them easy to watch. He adjusted the throttles and prop levers to match all four sets of needles, and saw the airspeed indicator creep up to 195 miles per hour. Archie looked ahead through the windshield, hoping to see land. The water was a featureless blur as it rushed by underneath. At that speed and low altitude, Archie had lost his depth perception. Unsure of how close to the water he really was, he kept the bomber just below the cloud layer and continued toward what he hoped would be England.

Walter Truemper rested for a short interval before something jarred him back to alertness. He was exhausted from the ordeal of the blind descent through the clouds. The searing pain from his frostbitten face and hands was almost unbearable, but he forced himself to concentrate on tuning the radio compass and plotting the signal courses on his chart. Truemper felt certain that they were nearing the English coast, and his radio position fixes supported that belief. He watched through the clear nose bubble, and after a while a thin, grey mass began to rise along the watery horizon up ahead. Within minutes the line was unmistakably land, but it still could not be positively identified. Truemper called the crew to stay alert as they approached the coastline.

The men aft of the cockpit had been able to relax slightly since flying out from beneath the clouds. They had not been fired upon by flak or fighters for some time, but the sighting of land caused the tension level to rise again. Russell Robinson, watching from the right waist window, was concerned about which country they might soon be over: "We made it back across the North Sea and sighted land, and hoped it was England. We crossed the coast, and made two circles overhead, then decided that it was friendly territory because nobody shot at us. We didn't know what country it was, though. It could have been Africa for all we knew, but we headed inland anyway."

Joe Rex hoped that they were over England, and tried to contact Polebrook. He had been having trouble tuning his receivers since the attack that had wounded him, but this was the first time he had tried to transmit. Rex's second call was to the cockpit, to report that more radio repair was needed before Ten Horsepower could summon help. Joe Rex explains: "The command set, the radio used for normal communication, had been shot out in the first attack. We needed to contact the base

Valor at Polebrook

for a heading report, and I had to use another transmitter to make the call. It didn't work at first, so I had to find the problem. I had this shrapnel in my arm, and it was really killing me. They had to do something, because I was working on the radios, so they gave me another dose of morphine. I got the set working, but my wounded hand was giving me trouble again."

With the threat of fighter attacks apparently over, Tom Sowell came up out of the ball turret and stood by to assist the radio operator: "Truemp called us in the radio room, and told us to get a QDM, so we'd know which way to fly. Joe's hand was hurt, so I had to help him. He told me which knobs to turn, and I turned those, and he eventually got the signal."

After a quick conference in the cockpit, Truemper, Mathies and Moore agreed that it would be best to get down as quickly as possible, even if it meant not landing at Polebrook. The first base they flew over was an RAF fighter field. Joe Rex called for permission to land: "We flew over a British base, and I told them we needed to land, but they refused after I had to explain that no experienced pilot was conscious to fly the landing attempt. There was talk about the British sending somebody up to check us out. They sometimes would be attacked by German crews flying captured American bombers. The Germans would come over with the returning stragglers, then go after targets in England. Apparently they decided we were a legitimate American crew, but they still wouldn't let us land."

Rex tried calling Polebrook again. The QDM request had been sent by Morse code, but this time Rex transmitted by voice. When the tower answered, Rex again asked for a heading to the base. Rex reported the course to Truemper, who climbed back up to the cockpit to instruct Sgt. Mathies to make the turn.

With rectangular patches of grey and brown farmland passing by close below, Archie Mathies was learning to really fly the B-17. Until this point, all any of the men needed to do was hold the big ship steady in course and altitude. Now, at low altitude over land, Mathies could instantly tell when the plane strayed from course. To Archie, it seemed that directional control was becoming more and more difficult. Both waist gunners reported the right aileron to be fluttering, and that the motion increased when Mathies tried to bank into even gentle turns. Archie tried making turns with rudder only, which resulted in very gradual changes of direction. Rapid maneuvers would be impossible due to the poor response from the damaged controls. Mathies dared not let up against the control column, as the nose would immediately come up and airspeed would drop dangerously. A stall at 1500 feet could mean sudden death for all on board.

The threat of fighter attack had passed, but there was still the danger of mid-air collision. The men at the windows had to stay alert, but Carl Moore was temporarily unable to help look for other airplanes. Whether it was from the unsteady flight at low level or from the built-up strain of all he had been through, Moore suddenly became violently airsick. He managed to move aft of his turret and lean into the bomb bay, but it took all his strength to remain standing against the force of his convulsions and the movement of the plane. Moore later related that for a short interval, he forgot all about the other problems on board: "I was so sick I didn't care much what happened to me."

Back to England

Lt. Truemper stood behind the armor plated seats and watched Archie Mathies try to stay in control of the crippled aircraft. There was much more talking going on now. Truemper did not have answers for all of the questions. He would have to get instructions from Polebrook. The implications of having damaged radios were now becoming apparent. With the command radio shot out, all calls to or from the plane would have to be relayed through Joe Rex, but Rex was badly wounded and could lose consciousness at any time. The young navigator climbed through the bomb bay and into the radio room. There was no standard procedure for what was about to happen. Walter Truemper would take that responsibility himself. He asked Sgt. Rex how to transmit with the jury-rigged equipment, put on the radioman's headset, and keyed the microphone.

The target area at Leipzig, February 20, 1944. The white streaks at left are from smoke canisters dropped to mark the target.

Valor at Polebrook

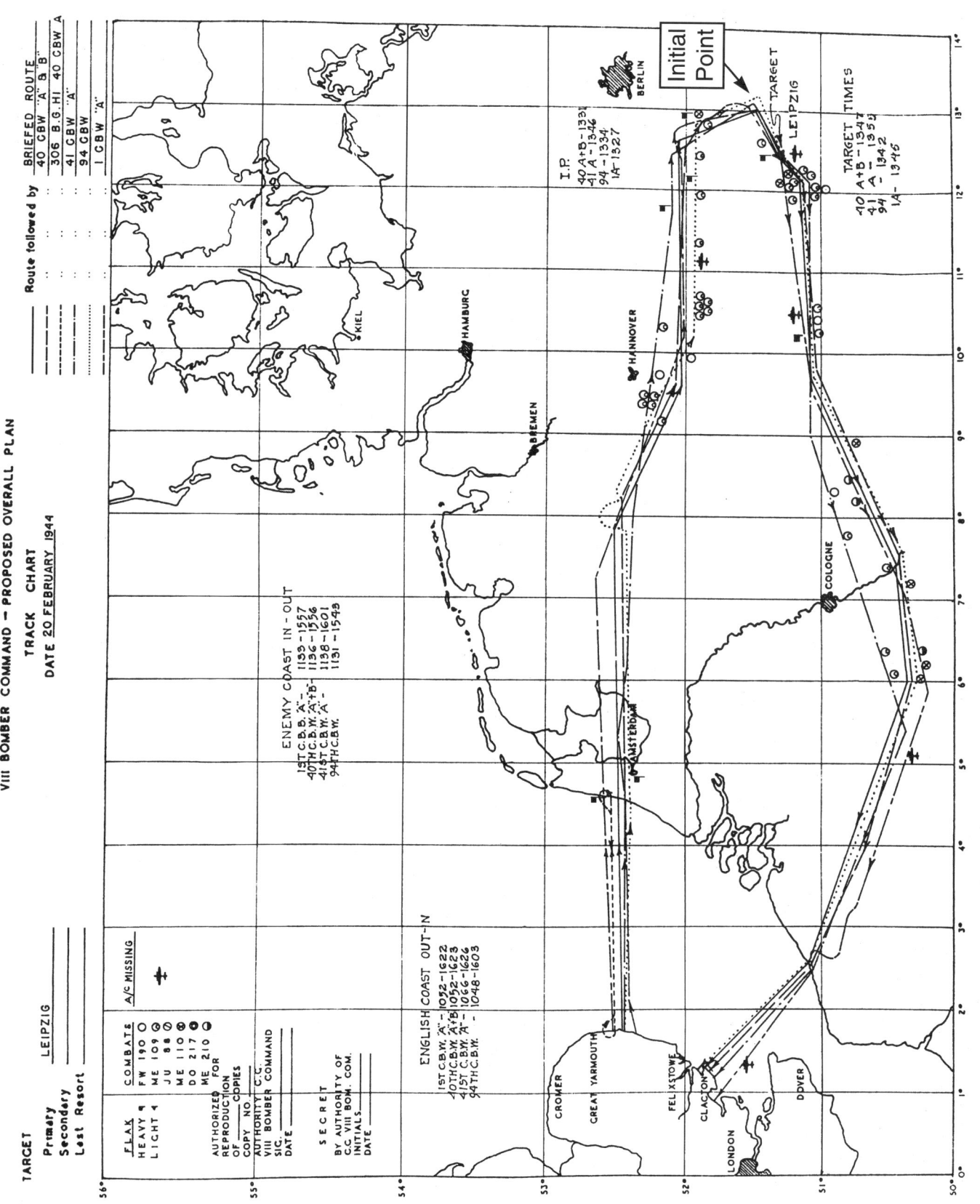

Navigation routes for the Leipzig mission. Note the Initial Point (IP) Northeast of Leipzig. Ten Horsepower was attacked prior to reaching this point.

Chapter Five: Landing

At 1533 on that dismal February Sunday, Polebrook tower operator Harold Flint was idle at his duty station. With the group not scheduled to return for another hour, Flint was not expecting any traffic at the base. The emergency that was soon to develop took him completely by surprise: "I was alone in the tower when all of a sudden over the (speaker) very loudly came this transmission asking for a heading to Polebrook. About ten minutes later there came another transmission and I heard a plane flying over the field. That transmission went like this: 'This is Paramount A-Able calling Newflick. The copilot is dead. The pilot we think is dead. The bombardier has jumped. I am the navigator, the only commissioned officer on board. What should we do?" Sgt. Flint told Truemper to stand by while he summoned a ranking officer. Flint set down the mic and picked up the phone to call for help.

Major Elzia Ledoux, commander of the 509th squadron, soon joined Sgt. Flint in the tower. Within minutes, Major Clinton Ball, Major Robert Burns and Colonel Eugene Romig, the base commander, reached the tower also. Sgt. Flint watched the lone bomber overhead, and wondered what was going on: "... the plane was circling the field, flying somewhat erratically, but it wasn't too bad a job of flying. At that time, there had been nothing said about who was flying the plane. (When the others arrived,) Burns took over the mic, and from then on I kept the log."

Details of the exchange between Lt. Truemper and Polebrook tower are vague, but the men on the ground soon understood that the flight engineer was flying "A-Able" (the 510th Squadron letter assigned to Ten Horsepower), and that there were wounded men on board. Lt. Truemper reported that he thought Sgt. Mathies would be able to land the plane with instructions from the tower. Col. Romig granted permission for the attempt. Russell Robinson and the others had already moved to the radio room to prepare for a landing: "When we got to Polebrook, Archie was planning on landing right away. He and Trump had decided that Archie could land the plane. When we got ready for a normal landing, we sat in the radio room with our backs toward the front of the plane. The ball turret was suspended from the top of the fuselage, right behind the radio room. On this landing, we packed flak jackets around it, because we thought the turret might break loose and crash into the radio room. There wasn't much else we could do. Still, we didn't think we weren't going to make it. I had no idea but that we were going to land and be OK. While we were up there, flying around, I couldn't visualize anything bad happening, because even though the plane was flying

Valor at Polebrook

A restored B-17 at the 1994 EAA airshow in Oshkosh, Wisconsin demonstrates with ease what Archie Mathies tried so desperately to do. Landing gear and flaps are down, propeller pitch is low, engine power at idle. Airspeed over the end of the runway: 90 miles per hour. (Photos by Jeff Rogers)

erratically, everything was going smoothly enough. But I realized how hard a plane hits the ground when it crash lands, and if the pilot doesn't get it right, the plane is going to fall to pieces. I've seen a lot of B-17s come in wheels up, or one wheel up, and hit the grass, and slide for four, five, six hundred yards before coming to a dead stop. Then everybody gets out. So I thought, it might be on the belly, and we might slide down the runway, but we'll be OK."

Alone in the cockpit, Archie Mathies had his hands full. He had plugged in his headset, and listened as Lt. Truemper relayed landing instructions from Polebrook tower. Mathies steered Ten Horsepower south of the field to come around and approach the northeast runway. This would bring the bomber onto a heading almost directly into the fifteen mile per hour wind. Archie pushed the right rudder pedal as hard as he could to hold the plane in the turn. The required pressure made his leg tremble so badly that he was afraid his muscles would cramp, but he was still worried about the damaged right aileron and didn't want to try a banking turn. Two miles from the end of the runway, Mathies relaxed rudder pressure and began to straighten the plane for the approach. He flipped the landing gear switch on the pedestal, and waited as the jackscrew in each inboard engine nacelle spun to lower the huge main wheels. Fifteen seconds passed before the green light above the gear switch glowed to show the wheels down and locked. Archie divided his attention between the runway and the flight

Landing

Even as he pulled back the throttles to try to drop the plane onto the ground, Mathies knew the landing attempt was going to fail. The Fortress did sink faster with power reduced, but the combination of excess airspeed, full flaps and ground effect kept the plane from settling. Archie watched as the far end of the runway widened in the windshield. He realized that if the plane did finally touch down, the big main wheels would roll onto the soft ground and sink in and the plane would flip over. Mathies' one-word comment was lost in the roar of the accelerating engines as he pushed the throttles forward and relaxed on the control yoke. The speeding plane climbed immediately. Archie moved the gear and flap switches to the "UP" position and watched the flight instruments. At fifteen hundred feet he pushed the wheel forward and held it there.

View looking forward past the waist guns to the ball turret. The door beyond opens into the radio room. Note control cables overhead. These continue forward through the radio room and into the bomb bay. (The Boeing Company Archives)

instruments above the pedestal. Ten Horsepower was still moving through the air at nearly two hundred miles per hour, and was not losing altitude as quickly as Mathies thought it would. He reached to the pedestal again, found the flap switch, and held it in the "DOWN" position. Each time Archie took one hand off of the control wheel, the nose lifted up, and he had to push harder with the hand still on the wheel to keep from climbing. When the flap position indicator showed full down flaps, Archie let go of the switch. The plane had slowed to 160 miles per hour, but this was still much too fast for a landing. With one hundred feet of air between aircraft and concrete, Ten Horsepower roared across the end of the runway.

Worried and frustrated at the missed landing, Archie Mathies held Ten Horsepower as steadily under control as he could. The failed attempt had given him a much better idea of how the plane would react during the landing. He was sure he could make it on the next pass. Archie's right leg began to ache from holding the rudder pedal in, and he finally gave up trying to keep the plane in a circle around the base. He concentrated on staying level below the clouds, and tried to keep Polebrook field in sight.

The officers watching from the ground were gravely concerned when Ten Horsepower throttled up and climbed away from the field. Col. Romig had to make decisions that would help the men stranded in the air, but he also had to consider the safety of the people on the ground. Even though Maj. Ledoux informed him that

Valor at Polebrook

neither Truemper nor Mathies had ever made a landing, Romig decided to allow them to remain on board but ordered them to circle around and have the rest of the crew bail out over the field before attempting to land again.

When Lt. Truemper repeated Col. Romig's orders, Sgt. Mathies looked over at the unmoving form in the pilot's seat. Archie wanted desperately to help his friend, but the only way he could would be to get the plane on the ground. The order to let the crew jump would mean more time had to pass before Lt. Nelson could get help, but Archie knew the others would be at risk if they remained on board. Mathies steered toward the field until he felt a turn would bring him parallel to the runway, but he misjudged the distance and overflew the strip. Cold and fatigue had dulled Archie's reactions. Without thinking, he rolled the wheel to the right as he pushed in the rudder pedal. The wavering bomber banked tightly, turning at a much faster rate than he had intended. Archie felt a strange vibration through the control column. His heart pounded from sudden fear of the damaged aileron falling off. In seconds, the plane was pointed back toward the runway. Mathies rolled the wings level, relaxed his pressure on the rudder pedal, and breathed out heavily in relief.

With the order for the gunners to jump came the instruction to climb as close to the clouds as possible, to give the men's parachutes more time to open. As he neared the field, Sgt. Mathies eased back on the wheel. Ten Horsepower quickly gained one hundred feet but entered some of the patchy clouds drifting below the overcast. Archie leveled off at 1600 feet and decided that was as high as he could climb without running into the clouds. Another shaky turn lined the plane up with the runway, then Archie held it as straight and level as he could. In the aft fuselage, the gunners were preparing to jump.

At the crew door just forward of the right horizontal stabilizer, Mac Hagbo found the emergency release handle and pulled. The door broke free and tumbled away in the slipstream. The men would jump as quickly as they could before the plane began moving away from the field. Joe Rex went out first: "The waist-gunners had given me more morphine, so by the time I had to bail out I was really a dead head. Tommy and Russ took my hand and wrapped it around the D-ring, set me in the door, and pushed me out. The air rushing by me apparently revived me and I jerked the chute open too soon. It was caught by the prop wash and one panel popped out. When the parachute opened, it jerked me so hard my boots came off. As I approached the ground I could see that I was going to land in a barbed wire entanglement, so I tried to guide myself the way I had seen paratroops do in the movies. I overdid it and dumped the chute about 40 feet up. I hit the ground with one foot on the hardstand, and the other foot in the mud, resulting in a triple fracture of my right ankle. But that was better than landing in the barbed wire, I think."

Russell Robinson jumped as soon as he thought Rex was clear of the plane: "When you're hanging up there in the air you're all to yourself. You don't hear anything, you're just floatin' like a bird. Really, you have no feeling of coming down, or anything. And then pretty soon you look down and, boy, you can see that ground coming up pretty fast. I could see that I was

Landing

coming down the wrong way, that I should turn my chute. They'd told us how to do that, to make your body float in a different direction. And I'd just gotten turned a quarter of the way around when I hit the ground, and all the weight was on my right foot. I didn't think it was really hurt, with my insulated electric boots on. While I was getting out of my harness, a farmer and his son who had seen me land came over and asked me if I was hurt. I told them I thought I had sprained my ankle, and if I had a stick or something to use as a crutch, I would be all right. I started to get up, but still couldn't make it. So, I asked the farmer for a cigarette. It wasn't but a few minutes until the ambulance came".

In the time needed to allow Rex and Robinson to jump, Ten Horsepower had crossed the airfield and was over the surrounding farmland again. Mathies turned the damaged bomber around as smoothly as he could, and made another pass to give the remaining gunners their chance to bail out. The plane wasn't quite over the field when Mac Hagbo jumped. He landed, uninjured, in the cemetery of a church near the base. Tom Sowell went out next, but wasn't as lucky as Hagbo. Sowell also broke a leg in landing.

Carl Moore was the last man to jump from Ten Horsepower. Before going aft to bail out, Moore shook hands with Archie Mathies and wondered if it would be the last time. Then he stepped past his top turret and climbed through the bomb bay and into the radio room. Walter Truemper looked up and smiled at his crew mate, and again Carl extended his hand. In that brief moment, each man silently asked God to

Tom Sowell's parachute is silhouetted against the overcast as he drifts down to a rough landing outside of Polebrook. February 20, 1944.

protect the other, and the two friends parted. Moore moved aft through the now empty fuselage to the open crew door. He turned and looked forward again. Through the open bulkheads of the radio room and bomb bay, Carl saw that Archie had turned around in his seat at the same instant. Moore gave the thumbs up, and Mathies returned the sign, but quickly turned back to the controls. Carl Moore took a deep breath, and moved to jump: *"I sat in the door, and was leaning out to see whether I would hit the stabilizer, when the slipstream jerked me out. I pulled the ripcord and floated down. At first I thought I was going to land on a bunch of sheep, and I thought that would be a nice spot. But I missed them."* Moore landed safely, was soon found, and was taken to the base dispensary.

Valor at Polebrook

Major Elzia Ledoux beneath a B-17F named after his wife. Note the escape hatch on the underside of the aircraft, the location from which Bombardier Joe Martin exited Ten Horsepower.

While the gunners were bailing out over the field, Major Ledoux and Colonel Romig drove to the 509th squadron dispersal area and climbed aboard the B-17 named My Princess, the flying spare that had turned back while still over the English Channel. Romig was all too familiar with wartime emergency landings. He had been awarded the Distinguished Flying Cross for helping to land another B-17 after its crew bailed out. On that flight, Romig had been on board the plane. This time, he would have to coach from the sidelines. The two officers wasted no time while starting the engines. Romig was in the right seat when Ledoux taxied out for take-off. By the time My Princess (RQ-Q, or "Q-Queenie" in military parlance) left the ground, Ten Horsepower was off to the south and turning around to line up for another approach to Polebrook. Maj. Ledoux narrates: "Col. Romig had informed Truemper and Mathies that he would be taking up another B-17 to try to talk them down, giving them instructions and hopefully confidence by flying alongside their aircraft. Romig, an engineer, and myself took off, and we caught up with their airplane, which was flying very erratically. We couldn't fly close formation with them, because collision was more of a probability than a possibility."

Col. Eugene Romig, Commander of the 351st Bomb Group on February 20th, 1944.

Sgt. Mathies was losing his struggle to keep Ten Horsepower in level, directed flight. Col. Romig later reported that it's airspeed fluctuated between 120 and 200 miles per hour, and that the crippled plane

Landing

B-17F 42-30499, My Princess, of the 509th Squadron. Major Elzia Ledoux and Col. Eugene Romig used this aircraft to assist Lt. Truemper and Sgt. Mathies during the attempts to land Ten Horsepower.

constantly climbed and dove around the 1600-foot mark. Ever wary of collision, Ledoux steered RQ-Q in as close as he could to determine how badly A-Able was damaged. Many small, jagged holes were visible on the vertical tail and aft right fuselage near the waist gunner's window. Several fist-sized puncture wounds in Joe Rex's skylight showed where the Focke-Wulf's shells had punched their way through. Two rows of dents and perforations from cannon strikes scarred the right wing. Areas of bent metal and shredded fabric could be seen on the right aileron. The aileron was fluttering rapidly and appeared to have had its control linkage shot away. The officers noted that all four engines were producing power and were not smoking, and that there did not appear to be any fuel leaking from the wing tanks. Ledoux had to stay alert as he scanned the familiar lines of the B-17, for Ten Horsepower could charge toward Q-Queenie without warning and bore right into them. Col. Romig suggested that it would be safer to observe from in front of A-Able, where there was less likelihood of collision. Major Ledoux smoothly banked RQ-Q and moved away to pull ahead of the faltering bomber. When they drew near again, the officers had their first good look at the cockpit area. The window directly above the copilot's seat was almost entirely shot away. Jagged-edged cracks could be seen in the copilot's side window, with a few smaller holes in the windshield. A frozen and exhausted Archie Mathies looked out through the fractured Plexiglas. He started to wave but quickly put his hand back on the control wheel as Ten

Valor at Polebrook

Horsepower jerked upward fifty feet. Mathies brought the plane back down slightly. Ledoux climbed to be level with it again, and looked over just as Walter Truemper's face appeared in the small, rectangular window above the right wing. Truemper and Mathies seemed alert and rational, but the expressions on their faces belied their fatigue. They had brought Ten Horsepower back to the field through pure determination. Ledoux and Romig could tell that the two were near the end of their endurance. Their fuel might be gone at any minute. Barely an hour of daylight remained, and the thick cloud cover would hasten the arrival of darkness. The field was clear of traffic for the moment, but the rest of the 351st would be returning from the mission soon. Time was running out.

Major Ledoux kept RQ-Q a safe distance from Ten Horsepower while Col. Romig called Lt. Truemper over the radio. Romig got no reply, and repeated his call. Truemper disappeared from the window briefly, then returned to look toward RQ-Q. For some reason, he was unable to hear Col. Romig's transmissions. Romig reached up to the radio control panel overhead to fine tune his Command set to 6440 kilocycles, then tried again. When this still brought no response from Truemper, Romig called Major Burns in the tower and asked if he was in contact with A-Able. Burns replied that Lt. Truemper had been calling RQ-Q, but then called the tower to ask for help with his radio. For the next several minutes, Burns and others radioed instructions to Walter Truemper in the hope that two-way communication could be established between Truemper and Romig. Walter was reluctant to change the settings on the transmitter for fear of losing contact with the tower. Gradually, it became understood that while Romig was using the Command radio, the set intended for short range contact, Truemper could only send and receive on the long range Liaison set, which was all that Joe Rex had been able to get working. Both sets could tune in 6440 kc, but small differences in the separate tuning circuits apparently prevented the radios from receiving each other. The only way left for Truemper and Romig to talk to each other was to call the tower and have the tower repeat the message to the other plane.

By now, Archie Mathies had Ten Horsepower almost lined up for another approach. Major Ledoux held RQ-Q steady and tried to lead Mathies down the glidepath: "Plane to plane radio communication proved to be impossible, so we relayed messages to them through the tower. We told them that we would try to guide them in for a landing. As we made the next approach, the landing looked like it was going to be accomplished. They were going right down the runway, but they still didn't seem to be able to slow the aircraft down enough to cause it to stall for the landing. So we went around again."

For the second time in twenty minutes, Archie Mathies had to accept the failure and climb back into the air. This time he had more than just one word for the howling slipstream tearing at his head, but the anger in his voice could not expel the fear tightening his stomach. Archie's arms and legs ached from fighting with the controls. His head and shoulders were chilled through, but beneath his flight suit he was wet from perspiration. To continue flying was agony. To give up would be sudden death. Shivering in his own sweat, Mathies held his weight against the rudder pedal and concentrated on following RQ-Q.

The sweeping turn which would bring the planes around for a third

Landing

approach took them very close to another bomber base south of Polebrook. Seeing this airfield, Molesworth, and observing that there was no traffic overhead at the time, Ledoux suggested a landing attempt there. Romig agreed, and RQ-Q turned south. Mathies followed. Maj. Ledoux states that the approach at Molesworth was "much more purposeful", as Sgt. Mathies seemed to be getting a better feel for handling the damaged plane. Even so, Ten Horsepower was still too high and Archie overshot the runway. With the throttles pulled back, the bomber soared down the centerline, settling slowly, but again ran out of room before running out of airspeed. Mathies throttled up and steered the ground-shy airplane into a climbing left turn. Major Ledoux continues: "Each time they missed a landing attempt, they pulled the gear back up. It was really up to them if they wanted to land gear down or up. They could have bellied it in, if they had wanted to, and I'm sure they'd have been OK. The flying field was grass, and even if they didn't land on the runway, the shoulders of the runway were grass. When we had people heading in for crash landings, we'd try to get them to parallel the runway instead of landing on it. It saved the runway from getting chewed up or closed while a wrecked airplane was dragged off. We had quite a number of planes land parallel to the runway, and most of them made out OK."

While Romig and Ledoux were trying to rejoin Ten Horsepower after the missed approach at Molesworth, Major Burns had to deal with the fact that the other 351st planes would soon be returning from their missions. With a crippled aircraft already having trouble getting down, Burns did not want the whole formation adding to the problem. He ordered the group to divert to Glatton, a field four miles to the east. Already over East Anglia, the 351st changed course for Glatton just as Ten Horsepower turned away from Molesworth.

Col. Romig had taken a chance in allowing Truemper and Mathies to stay with their aircraft. After watching two failed landing attempts, he was convinced that there was no way the untrained airmen could get the damaged plane safely back on the ground. As Ten Horsepower climbed after the missed landing at Molesworth, Romig told Lt. Truemper to point the plane toward the North Sea, set the automatic pilot, and bail out. Even before Romig had finished his instruction, Walter Truemper was wrestling with his conscience. He had to make the most important decision of his life, and had little time to reason. Lt. Nelson was definitely still alive. The thought of leaving him was unthinkable, yet Truemper was being told to do exactly that. He knew that if the autopilot was turned on, the plane would dive toward the ground. He and Mathies might not have time to jump clear before it crashed. Walter Truemper was always able to think on his feet however, and he responded like the levelheaded professional he was. After only a brief discussion with Archie, Truemper answered that he and Mathies would jump if they were being ordered to, but that they still thought they could get the plane back down. Truemper went on to explain the problem with the auto-pilot, then waited for a reply. A tense silence filled the navigator's headset while Col. Romig reconsidered. Moments later, Romig granted permission for another attempt.

Reasons for what happened next are not clear. Although Ledoux and Romig intended to return to Polebrook after the failed landing at Molesworth, Ten

Valor at Polebrook

Horsepower strayed off in the direction of Glatton. It is possible that in his frustration Sgt. Mathies became disoriented. Each of his circles around Polebrook were made in the right-hand direction, but his pattern at Molesworth turned to the left. This may have confused Archie, for he steered away from the field before RQ-Q could move ahead of him to lead him back to Polebrook. Major Ledoux states that Ten Horsepower got very close to Glatton, but didn't actually make a landing attempt there: "When we headed toward Glatton, we didn't see any airplanes because they had not returned from the mission yet. But just as we were coming in toward that base, Glatton tower started firing flares. We looked out in the distance and the (diverted 351st) formation was coming in to make their landings. For fear of interfering with those landings, we decided to head back to Polebrook."

Archie Mathies turned Ten Horsepower away from Glatton, and did not disrupt the approaching formation, but time had run out. Col. Romig's official report of these events, filed on February 22, 1944, describes Ten Horsepower's final moments: *"...There was no further recourse but to attempt to assist A-Able to land, but apparently instructions to follow Q-Queenie were not understood, or could not be followed. One attempt was made by A-Able to crash land at Molesworth. Flaps were lowered, and airspeed slowed to normal. However, he overshot badly and realizing it, went around. Instructions were relayed for A-Able to return to Polebrook for any landing attempts, as the Airdrome had been cleared of traffic and prepared for emergency landing. A-Able headed North as directed, but missed Polebrook and joined heavy traffic at Glatton. At this time, Q-Queenie was following about 75 to 100 yards behind at 180 to 190 mph. As A-Able apparently joined traffic at Glatton, he suddenly veered off to the left in a sweeping diving turn past the tower, which, believing him attempting to land, shot red flares. He headed for an open field a mile or so away. As the aircraft neared the ground, the throttles were cut back, as evidenced by the flare-back from the turbos, apparently in an attempt to make a normal crash landing, but the aircraft hit at an indicated speed of 200 mph at a slightly nose-down attitude at 1700 hours. It skidded along the ground for 50 yards or more, then hit a mound of dirt and cartwheeled and broke to pieces."*

Maj. Ledoux describes the crash as seen from RQ-Q: "On the way back to Polebrook, we noticed a very large, open field. It was in a hilly part of the terrain, but Mathies headed the aircraft directly for this field, and we breathed a sigh of relief. We figured that he could very well make a landing in an open field, but their approach wasn't good. Being experienced pilots, Romig and I could tell that they were headed to land up-hill. We tried to guide them toward the down gradient of this field so they could land downhill instead of uphill. In fact, we were both yelling at them at the top of our lungs even though we knew they couldn't hear us. Apparently wanting to get the aircraft down as soon as possible, Sgt. Mathies headed into the upgrade. He flared out, and it seemed he was going to make a good landing, but the nose dug into this God-awful hill and the aircraft disintegrated. Romig and I were near enough that had the plane violently exploded, we probably would have been hit by some of the flying debris. It was a very sad and shocking sight for both of us. Neither of us said a word for an indefinite time after that..."

Landing

The wreckage of Ten Horsepower, a silent testimony to the violence of the crash. Denton Hill, February 20th, 1944.

Valor at Polebrook

Many of the people involved in the efforts to help Mathies and Truemper have speculated on what might have happened during those final moments. It is possible that Ten Horsepower ran out of fuel, but it is very unlikely that all four engines would have quit at the same time. The fact that the plane did not explode and the absence of a post-crash fire clearly show that there was very little fuel in the tanks. Archie Mathies was undoubtedly exhausted from his extended time at the controls in the open cockpit. Some say he had had enough, and thought the field would give him ample distance in which to bleed off airspeed and let the plane settle in on its belly, but Maj. Ledoux recalls that the gear were in the down position as Mathies approached the hill. Interviews with the gunners who bailed out of Ten Horsepower suggest that the damaged control cables in the bomb bay finally failed completely, sending the plane plunging uncontrollably toward the ground. It is a certainty that the elevator controls were damaged, as evidenced by the need for constant forward pressure on the control column during the flight home and the landing attempts. The "flare back from the turbos" as witnessed by Ledoux and Romig could only have resulted from a deliberate and sudden reduction of power, as if the throttles were instantly pulled back in a desperate attempt to slow the aircraft for a landing. The exact cause of the crash will never be known, for Walter Truemper and Archie Mathies died instantly when Ten Horsepower tore itself to pieces across the face of the hill.

Ronald Bartley's short-snorter, the two-dollar bill signed by his crewmates upon arrival in Ireland. Visible signatures include C.R. Nelson, W.E. Truemper, M.A. Hagbo, C.W. Moore, Archie Mathies, and Joe F. Rex. December 17, 1943.

Chapter Six:
On the Ground

News of Ten Horsepower's dilemma had not yet traveled across Polebrook when Archie Mathies lined up for his first approach. It was not uncommon for aircraft crippled during a mission to return early, so the appearance of a lone B-17 didn't attract much attention. There was no hint that anything was out of the ordinary, until the plane climbed away without touching down. When the plane's first pass was unsuccessful, those watching expected it to go around to line up for another attempt. Instead, the damaged bomber circled higher over the field, and parachutes began to billow open behind it. At the same time, a staff car sped along the perimeter track. Two officers got out, and within minutes another B-17 was streaking down the runway to join the circling aircraft. This *was* uncommon, and the curious onlookers began to realize that a significant aerial drama was being played out in the sky above them. Few people on the ground knew what was going on, but the basic facts were obvious: The aircraft was badly shot up, and was difficult to control. A safe landing seemed unlikely.

Naturally, the people working in Polebrook tower during the landing efforts were much better informed. Anyone close by could hear the radio transmissions. The flurry of activity among the ranking officers heightened the sense of urgency. James Waitt, a weather officer on duty that day, recalls the scene in the tower: "The weather office was on the ground floor of the control tower, with the radio room and tower operators directly above on the second floor. The weather office ran the width of the building, with windows at both ends. The entire west wall had casement windows running from two feet above the floor up to the ceiling. With the blackout curtains pushed back in the daytime, we had an excellent view of the runways.

The control tower at Polebrook airfield. Sgt. Harold Flint's duty station was on the second floor. Weather Officer James Waitt watched the landing attempts from behind the large casement windows on the lower level.

Valor at Polebrook

"When the control tower operators said the planes would be returning from Leipzig, I started sending up weather reports every fifteen minutes. The medics, and the crash crews with their asbestos suits on, were at their stations just south of the control tower with the motors of the crash trucks running. This was the usual procedure for mission landings as some of the planes would be in trouble due to battle damage and would have wounded aboard.

"When word came down from flying control that one of our planes was coming in with no pilot or co-pilot, things became more hectic than usual. When I had a few seconds away from my duties, I looked outside to try to see the plane coming in. About the time I spotted it, the remaining crew were ordered to bail out. I watched the plane, which at that time was about three quarters of a mile west of the tower, heading in a southerly direction at a relatively low altitude. I saw some parachutes open, and the plane proceeded on south.

"I heard that two crewmembers were going to try to land the plane. In a few minutes, I saw them coming in on the final approach. From the control tower, about 300 feet north of the main runway, everything looked good. I thought they were going to make it, but they apparently were not lined up with the runway, and they passed over at about 100 feet. At the same time, the commanding officer of the base was flying alongside trying to talk them down. The planes came around for a second attempt, but could not get lined up. Then they flew about the same route they had when the crewmembers jumped, but were a little farther out from the tower. I watched them disappear to the south, and didn't see them again. About an hour later, I learned of the sad ending for such brave and gallant airmen."

The men waiting in the rescue vehicles had seen emergency landings before, but none had ever seen untrained crewmen try to land their plane. Sgt. William Vorhies, an ambulance driver, found the arrival of Ten Horsepower anything but routine: "Normally, when the group was returning, we'd line up the ambulances near the end of the runway. When the planes came in, they'd shoot off red flares if they had wounded on board. We'd drive out and direct the planes. They'd come over close to us, and we'd get in and get the wounded out.

"While we were waiting there, I saw the Major (Ledoux) and the Colonel (Romig) hot foot it out from the tower to go out and get another plane. I watched them take off to try to help get (Truemper and Mathies) down. While this was happening, the damaged plane had circled over the base and the crewmen began to parachute down. They didn't all jump at once, and they scattered every which way. There were ambulances, jeeps, fire trucks, everything we had going after them. Everybody was out there trying to pick them up. It was very hectic. There was a lot of excitement. Everybody wanted to be sure they were all right, naturally. We picked up one of the first ones to jump. He had landed off base, closer to Polebrook, to the west. He hadn't been hurt, but I don't remember his name.

"After they had all jumped, the plane kept circling the base, just over and around, back and around, back again. They were trying to get down, and trying to get down, and trying, but neither one of them had ever landed a plane. All of the circling added to the tension. It was a good thirty minutes or so before they left our airspace to head for another base. Of course later we learned what had happened after that. I'll tell you, they're the two most heroic young men that you could ever

On the Ground

THE FLYING FORTRESS WHICH FAILED TO LAND BEING COACHED BY THE STATION C.O. FROM THE LOWER FORTRESS.
The navigator and ball-turret gunner brought a Flying Fortress back from a raid over Germany with the pilot unconscious and the co-pilot killed. The Station C.O., in another Fortress, tried to coach the two men to make a landing. Unhappily, they crashed, and were killed.

The photo carried for years afterward by Michael Balkovich appeared in an English newspaper soon after the mission. (Illustrated London News Picture Library photo.)

visualize. They just wanted to save their pilot."

For many years after the war, Michael Balkovich, an Intelligence officer with the 508th squadron, carried in his wallet a photo of two B-17s flying almost alongside each other. Taken from the ground, the picture shows Ten Horsepower and My Princess as they passed over Polebrook during the landing effort. Lt. Balkovich comments: "We at Polebrook did not see the actual crash, as the attempted landing was at an airfield several miles away. Some of us watched the drama from the top of the Polebrook control tower. The two aircraft circled the area for quite some time, providing Col. Romig a chance to give Mathies and Truemper a quick course in landing a B-17. During this interval, the photo was taken.

"The very simplicity of the photo does not generate much interest to the average person. However, to some of us it represents the heroic and tragic drama going on inside the aircraft at the time. It is one of the most dramatic photographs I have ever seen.

"Incidents of courage, sacrifice, devotion to duty, and heroism which today would make front page headlines were then so commonplace that they received fleeting recognition in that violent existence. Even the actions of Truemper and Mathies were soon forgotten, as the days that followed were only more of the same. Those of us who watched the landing attempt and subsequent crash from a distance will always consider this the ultimate example of valor, but at the time we had little chance to reflect upon it, as each new day would bring other incidents that would dominate our thoughts."

Onlookers at Polebrook could know only what they saw as the two planes circled overhead, but the plight of the stricken bomber had been reported to neighboring airbases. The British were also tracking Ten Horsepower as it meandered across their countryside. Mr. Arthur Pettifor was one of the Englishmen who became involved in the event and actually saw the plane crash: "During the war years, I was a member of the Royal Observer Corps. We were the 'Eyes and Ears' of the Royal Air Force. Observer Posts were positioned about fifteen miles apart throughout East Anglia, and each Post had a direct line to a Center in Cambridge which in turn was in constant touch with R.A.F. Fighter Command and all of the airbases.

Valor at Polebrook

"I was assigned to the Observation Post on a hilltop at Sawtry, approximately two miles south of Denton. During the afternoon of February 20, I was on duty with a colleague. The Center at Cambridge informed us that a B-17 bomber returning to Polebrook from a raid over Germany had been severely damaged by enemy gunfire, and requested us to concentrate on the movement and action of this aircraft. After accepting it from a neighboring Post at Ramsey, to the east, I proceeded to plot its position continually. The instruments we used indicated the exact square mile the aircraft was over at any given time, and this information was relayed to the Center.

"I plotted the aircraft on its way to Polebrook Base and then for some time as it circled around. Several parachutes were seen to fall. It then flew over Molesworth Base and eventually headed in an easterly direction, passing over Glatton Air Base towards the Fens. Before reaching the town of Ramsey, it turned back in a westerly direction towards Polebrook. As the aircraft approached the A1 main road, it was losing height and narrowly missed a belt of trees parallel to the road. I could see that it would not clear a hill between the A1 road and Denton village. The plane hit half way up the hill and disintegrated in a large cloud of dust. I did not see any fire. Fire tenders and rescue teams from Glatton, Polebrook, and elsewhere were soon on the scene, but I did not visit the site."

An English civilian also witnessed the crash, and he did visit the site, as the airplane practically came down on top of him. Reginald Griffin tells this story: I was raised at a place called Moonshine Gap, right in the middle of the air bases, so we saw the B-17s every day going out and coming back, some with engines stopped, holes in their tails, etc. My first job after leaving school in 1942 was at Polebrook airfield working for a construction company. I was only fourteen at the time. I later worked at Glatton airbase with the same company. My mother used to do laundry for some of the boys that I got to know during my work, and she did such a good job that I was kept busy evenings and weekends. I used to fetch and carry laundry on my old bicycle, which I had to walk with most of the time due to the load. It was on one of these trips to Glatton on a Sunday afternoon that I witnessed the crash. I was about 800 meters down the lane from the gate opening onto the field that is Denton Hill when I saw and heard the bomber sweeping in very low from the Glatton side of the A1 main road. It looked like it was trying to make a belly landing. It just cleared some tall trees and high-tension cables, and I realized it was going to crash. The plane hit the deck approximately 400 meters from the A1 road. There was a small piece of ploughed land adjacent to the main road, then a small hedgerow, which the plane hit. It careened up the hill toward the trees at what looked like a hell of a speed to me, then hit the ground again. The plane broke up completely, with the main part of the wreckage in and at the tree line. It was unbelievable, and so quick!

"I ran as fast as I could up the hill. Bits of the airplane were strewn across the slope. I saw a pair of legs dressed in flying suit trousers protruding from some of the wreckage. I saw the body of another crewmember lying face downwards beneath a broken branch. I went close to him, but did not touch him. As far as I could see, he was unmarked and his clothes were not torn. He was a young man. I was the only one there for about fifteen minutes, until the Military Police arrived. Then I ran away."

On the Ground

In contrast to the speed and violence of the crash, Reginald Griffin found only silent wreckage on Denton Hill.

Mrs. Doris Whitaker, a resident of Denton, was outside of her home when Ten Horsepower passed overhead on its way to Polebrook: "We were facing west when the plane first went by, then we saw it again with the other plane that was trying to talk it down. A very few minutes later, U.S. Military Police and all sorts of cars and other vehicles came rushing by, and we knew there must have been a crash, but we saw no fire."

Rescuers were on the scene very quickly after the crash, but there was little for them to do. Sgt. Mathies and Lt. Truemper had been killed instantly by the force of the impact. Amazingly, Lt. Nelson was still alive when the crash crew found him in the wreckage. Nelson was immediately taken to the base hospital. In the failing light of the mid-winter evening, with the temperature falling back down below the freezing mark, the bodies of Truemper, Mathies, and Flight Officer Bartley were recovered and placed in an ambulance for their final ride to Polebrook.

Mr. Griffin and Mrs. Whitaker both state that personal cameras were practically unheard of during the war, and that no one took any pictures. The only known photographs of the wreckage at the crash site were taken by the U.S. military before the clean-up work began. For three days, salvage crews collected and removed as much of the remains of Ten Horsepower as they could. Some of the debris was deeply imbedded in the soft ground on the hillside. Numerous small pieces were left scattered in and among the trees, as were some pieces purposely thrown there and forgotten. With the coming of spring and

Valor at Polebrook

Looking northeast toward Denton Hill as it appeared in Spring of 1992. Ten Horsepower first touched down in an open area off to the right of this view, bounded upward over a large hedgerow, then crashed and tumbled uphill toward the trees at the center of the photo.

the sprouting of new foliage, all remaining traces of '763 were hidden.

None of the men who bailed out over Polebrook had any idea of what had happened at Denton Hill. By the time they reached the ground, Ten Horsepower was out of sight to the south. Sergeants Robinson, Sowell, and Rex each made very hard landings with their parachutes, and were each taken to the base hospital as soon as they were picked up. For Joe Rex, the process took slightly longer. Rex's flying suit had been smeared with blood while he helped move the copilot. The first medic to reach Rex thought he had been badly wounded in the chest. Rex was in great pain from his shattered ankle, and had no idea how he must have looked to the attendant, who was trying to open Joe's flight suit to dress the non-existent wound. Rex kept begging the man to look at his broken leg. Finally, the medic picked up the leg, gave it a twist, and said 'This leg isn't broken.' Joe nearly passed out from the pain. He managed to pull his .45 from its holster and point it at the well intentioned rescuer. Rex told the man that if he didn't put the leg down, Rex was going to shoot. As Joe recalls, "I think he believed me, because he put it down and ran away." It was a very cautious group of medics who finally put Rex on a stretcher and loaded him into the ambulance.

The three injured gunners were reunited at the base hospital, where Tom Sowell realized that he had "broken" more than just his leg: "When I bailed out, my parachute straps were too loose around my legs. They came up and caught my testicles. Boy, I was hurting. I didn't urinate until the next afternoon. I'll tell you, I bailed out two times: My first and my last.

"After I landed, I was rolled up in my parachute in the wet grass. It was sleetin' and snowin', and I was cold. I heard some guys talking and I started hollering at them. They were out bird hunting. They took off their shotgun barrel and made a splint and tied my legs together. They found a jeep and put me across the back of it and started to drive me to the hospital. But

On the Ground

then they ran through this old wooden gate, and the barrel of the shotgun hit the gate post and pulled me off the jeep. I was lyin' there, with my parachute across the jeep, and they almost left me there. But they turned around and came back.

"The two guys that brought me in had to take the first jeep they could find. It so happened that the one they took belonged to the Provost Marshall. Well, they got caught, and had to explain why they took his jeep. The next day, the Provost Marshall brought those two into the hospital for me to identify as the guys who had helped me. He said if I could identify them, they wouldn't be in any trouble. I didn't really remember, but I thought I recognized one of the two, so I said it was them."

Joe Rex's wounded arm and hand required three operations before they could begin to heal. His ankle was fractured so badly that he would spend many weeks in recovery and physical therapy. Sgt. Rex was sedated during the first days of his hospitalization. Officers from Polebrook Airbase questioned him briefly on the evening of the crash, then left to let him rest.

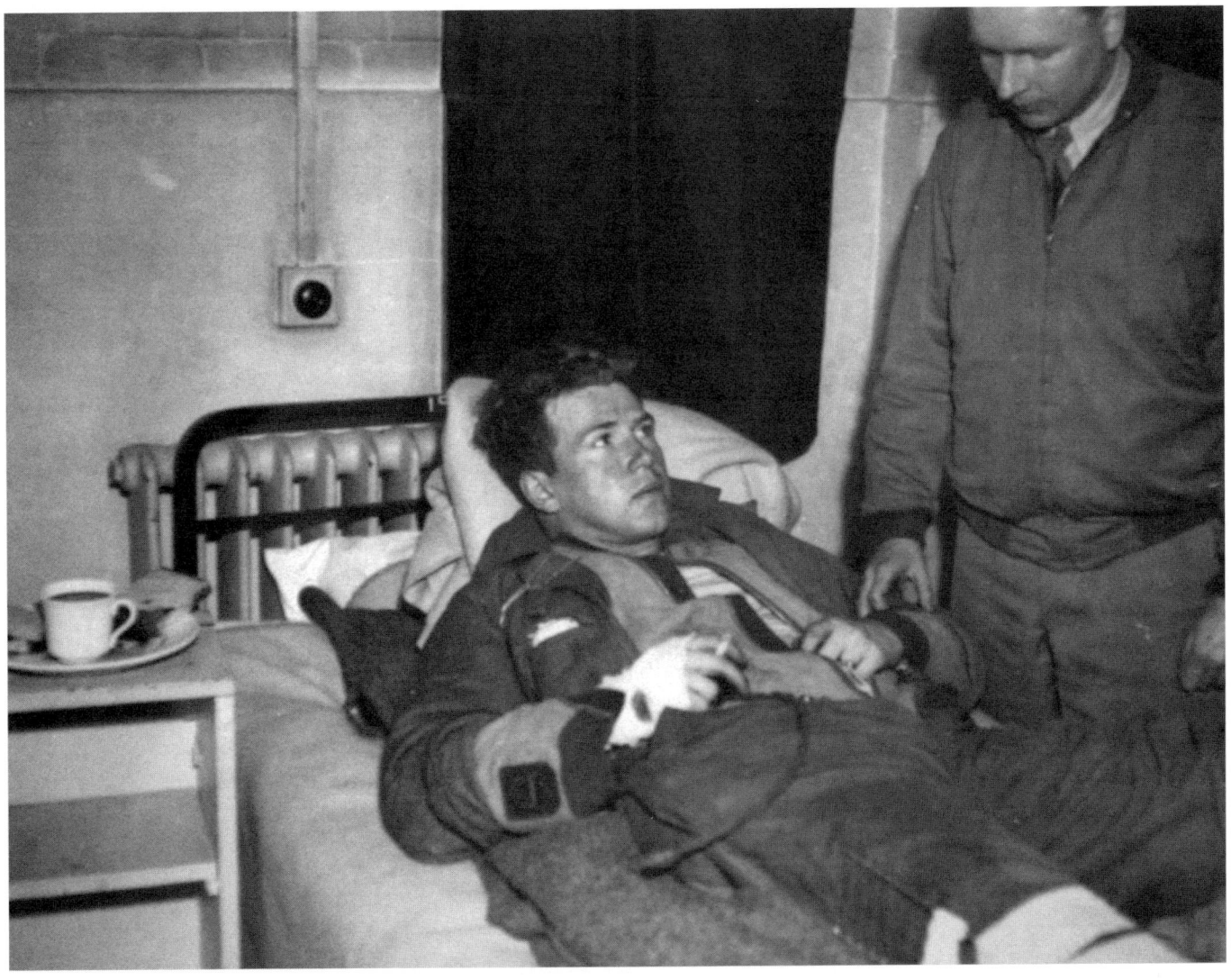

Joe Rex in the hospital after the mission. Rex's wounds improved quickly after the shrapnel was removed, but required multiple surgeries before healing could begin.

Valor at Polebrook

Russell Robinson in the hospital after the mission.

After his ambulance ride, Russell Robinson found himself in a crowded corridor, waiting for a doctor: "The hospital they took us to was used by the infantry too. It wasn't just for the air force. With all the casualties coming in, the place was pretty busy. I had to lay out in the hall on a cot and wait my turn to see the doctors, because they were taking care of other people hurt a lot worse than I was. I laid there for what seemed like an hour. I was getting cold, shivering and shaking. I got another blanket from a nurse who came by once in a while. She was a big, jolly gal. She kept saying they'd be by to pick me up soon and get me fixed up. They finally took me into a room and set my leg and put a cast over it. The bone was cracked, and it hurt. They moved me to a big, long room with lots of beds. Some of them were curtained off. There were a bunch of other people, many of them soldiers. Joe and Tommy were there too. Our beds were right next to each other. We were wondering what had happened to the others. We hadn't heard anything. Later that night, Carl and Mac came in to see us. They told us Archie and Wally hadn't made it, and that Lt. Nelson had died from his injuries after reaching the hospital."

When Truemper and Mathies were ordered to bail out even though Lt. Nelson was still alive, they decided without hesitation that they would not abandon him to save themselves. Trying to land the damaged plane was a gamble they chose to take, and if they had made it the gamble would have paid off. In recalling the events of February 20th, Major Louis Nowack, the 351st Group Medical Officer, stated that Lt. Nelson could have survived the wounds he received in combat if Ten Horsepower had landed safely at Polebrook. But it was not to be, and as the news of Lt. Nelson's death sank in, the five gunners realized that half of their crew had been lost that day.

On Monday, February 21st, many English newspapers ran stories about the tragic loss of two brave American airmen. Among those reading the accounts was twenty-one year old David Mathies, Archie's younger brother. David Mathies was an aircraft armorer with the 4th Fighter Group. The news caught him completely by surprise: "I remember February 20th very well, as the bombers from nearby Bassingbourne Airfield were out early, circling over our base. The crew chiefs were out on the flight line warming up the fighters' engines. It was the start of the "Big Week". I was apprehensive all day long, because I knew Archie would probably be up for the mission. The 20th passed without incident, and the next day too. That evening, I went to the Red Cross building for a cup of tea, and I picked up a newspaper. There on the front page was the whole story. I couldn't believe what I was reading. Archie dead? It couldn't be true, but it was. I immediately requested

On the Ground

emergency leave. I arrived at Polebrook the next day. I spoke with Col. Romig, and other officers, and was given a copy of the official action report detailing the events of my brother's last mission. I was taken to the infirmary, where I met Joe, Russell, and Tom, who had bailed out over the base. We talked for a while, and they told me what had happened on the plane. Finally I was taken to the building where they kept the belongings of those who were killed in action. I collected a few of Archie's things, to send home. I spent that night in the crew's barracks, and went back to my base the next day."

Mac Hagbo, back at Polebrook following his parachute landing.
Mac has just been told that his crewmates have crashed.

IN RECOGNITION OF VALOR AND MERITORIOUS SERVICE

The heroism and sacrifice of February 20, 1944 did not go unrecognized. Nelson's crew received two Medals of Honor, one Distinguished Service Cross, one Silver Star, and seven Purple Hearts. At the cost of four lives, the men of Ten Horsepower became the most decorated crew to fly with the Eighth Air Force in World War II.

THE MEDAL OF HONOR

The Medal of Honor is The United States' highest military decoration. It is awarded for conspicuous gallantry and intrepidity at the risk of life, above and beyond the call of duty, in action involving actual conflict with an opposing armed force.

The Medal of Honor originated during the Civil War. It can only be awarded by an act of Congress and the order of the Commander in Chief.

THE DISTINGUISHED SERVICE CROSS

The Distinguished Service Cross is the second highest military honor bestowed by the U.S. Government. Instituted in 1918, the Distinguished Service Cross is awarded for extraordinary heroism in action against an enemy of the United States while engaged in military operations involving conflict with an opposing foreign force or while serving with friendly foreign forces.

THE SILVER STAR

The Silver Star was instituted by the War Department in 1932. Ranked fifth of the fifteen medals given for valor and meritorious service, the Silver Star is awarded for gallantry in action against an armed enemy of the United States or while serving with friendly foreign forces.

THE PURPLE HEART

The Purple Heart evolved from the Badge of Military Merit which was designed by General George Washington in 1782. The War Department revived the design in 1932 as the Purple Heart and directed that it be awarded to any member of the U.S. Armed Forces who is killed or wounded in an armed conflict. George Washington's profile appears on the heart shaped pendant.

Chapter Seven: Post Mission, Post War

Despite the loss of Ten Horsepower and other aircraft on February 20th, the "Big Week" raids continued. This meant business as usual for the 351st. On four of the next five days, the Triangle J could be seen over Germany. None of the Ten Horsepower survivors flew on the remaining February missions. With three of the five gunners injured, it would be weeks before the men would see action again.

Joe Rex's ankle was broken so badly that he was forced to remain hospitalized for several months. Two weeks after being wounded, Rex was able to begin using a wheelchair to move around. His hand had healed enough to allow him to write again, but with difficulty and only for short periods at a time. On March 10th, while on an inspection tour of the hospital, Eighth Air Force officers presented Sgt. Rex with the Purple Heart. Later that day, he was visited by John Morris, Rex's cousin who worked in London as a photographer for LIFE magazine. In a letter to Joe's parents, Morris tried to reassure them that their son would be all right. He related the basic events of February 20th, stated that Joe had "stood the psychological strain of the whole business well," and added that Rex was "very cheerful."

Sgt. Joe Rex displays his Purple Heart after his release from the hospital.

Joe Rex's efforts in helping Ten Horsepower return to Polebrook did not go unrecognized. On March 20th, 1944, he was awarded the Silver Star. In part, his citation read, "Sergeant Rex's devotion to duty in the face of great obstacles helped to make possible the airplane's return to its base and the saving of five lives. His

Valor at Polebrook

courageous conduct on this occasion reflects highest credit upon himself and the Armed Forces of the United States."

Rex was eventually able to return to his squadron: "I was still in the hospital on D-Day. I was released so long after that that I never did fly combat again. I did fly a couple of high altitude weather missions over Europe. Then after the war, I made three trips to Lenz, Austria, to fly French prisoners back to Paris. Some of those French soldiers had been in prison camps for seven years. They had been horribly mistreated. They looked just awful.

"After VE Day, many of the B-17s were flown back to the States. About the time I was supposed to go home, I heard about a crew that needed a radio operator. I decided that I'd much rather fly back than go home on a ship, so I signed on with them. They took twenty personnel on each plane, instead of the usual ten. We flew to Iceland, and on to Connecticut. From there I traveled by train. My brother was a navigator on an Air/Sea Rescue B-17 based in Tampa, Florida. I had a thirty-day leave, so I went down to see him. I rode along on one of his flights while I was there. That's the last time I flew on a B-17. I started to train with a B-29 outfit, but the war ended before I was needed in the Pacific."

In 1945, Joe Rex returned to his home town of Defiance, Ohio. Joe's interest in radio had shifted from the technical aspects to the employment opportunities in network broadcasting. Taking advantage of the GI Bill, he enrolled at Heidleburg College in Tiffin, Ohio as a student of broadcast journalism. After college, Joe's marriage ended. In time, he renewed his friendship with a woman he met at Heidleburg. They were married in 1952. In 1955, Joe and Margaret Rex moved to Peoria, Illinois, where Joe went to work as a

November 11, 1989 - Joe Rex holds the four .50 caliber shells removed from his radio room gun.

newscaster with radio station WMBD. Three sons and thirty years later, Joe retired to private life in Peoria.

One of Joe Rex's most treasured souvenirs is a section of an ammunition belt which holds four .50 caliber bullets. These four shells were recovered from his radio room machine gun after the plane had crashed, and were given to Rex by one of the clean-up crew. Joe explains why these bullets mean so much to him: "The plane that wounded me came in from straight above us. Normally, Carl Moore would have been in the top turret, but he was helping to fly the plane at the time, so his turret was unmanned. The waist guns wouldn't raise up high enough, so I was the only gunner who could get a shot at the fighter. I fired until I thought I had run out

Post Mission, Post War

of ammunition, but I later found out my gun had jammed. These bullets were all the ammo I had left, and they're all I have to show for the FW 190. He got me, and I got him, but the Air Force never gave me credit for shooting him down.

Citizen Joe Rex displays the Silver Star, Purple Heart, and campaign ribbons he earned as a Sergeant in the U.S. Army Air Corps during World War II.

"I don't know if anyone on board the plane saw the FW blow up. We were never debriefed about that part of the mission. All the talk was about the landing efforts. The officers never did seem to figure out just how I got wounded, or how the radio gear got shot up. I have always wanted to pursue this with the higher powers, because I'm sure I shot down a FW 190. Having that confirmation would mean more to me than the Purple Heart and the Silver Star. I had thoughts of trying to work through the German Air Force, but I haven't ever had the time or energy to do all of the detective work involved." Joe Rex never did get the credit he wanted. In the early morning hours of August 29th, 1995, after a hard-fought battle against a lengthy illness, he passed away in his sleep.

Russell Robinson demonstrates the proper fitting of a chest-pack parachute. Crewmen practiced emergency exit procedures in the B-17 fuselage in the background. Note the cast still on Russell's right leg.

Winter ended quietly for Russell Robinson, who spent six weeks on the ground while his leg healed. Russell had been injured while bailing out due to enemy action, but for some reason did not receive the Purple Heart. It did not occur to him to

Valor at Polebrook

ask why, and he did not pursue the matter. In April, Robinson was assigned to fly as a replacement gunner for other crews. When not flying, he worked as an aircraft armourer and mechanic. Robinson logged a total of thirteen missions before war's end.

Russell took a lot of teasing about a story that had started to circulate. It seemed that he was sending all of his money home so his wife could buy a tractor to make her farm work easier. Russell says the real story turned out to be more interesting: "My wife was learning how to fly. She was flying when I got home, and she had bought an airplane. I didn't know anything about this. She had helped to start a flight school, with instructors and airplanes.

"I learned to fly after I got home. I enjoyed it. We bought a few more of the planes that our instructors and military pilots had learned to fly in, the AT-6. We all learned how to fly. My sisters flew, and my brother had been a liaison pilot in the Pacific. When he came back, he had a commercial license. He worked for an outfit that was buying Army surplus planes in Texas, and he'd fly them to our field as a stopover point. He'd fly them in here and leave them for a few days. We'd get some old boy's airplane and fly the tar out of it. We'd fly everything that came in. We had a lot of fun, but some people got killed, too. One guy took a trainer up in bad weather and ran it into the ground.

"We had a good time with the school. A lot of people learned to fly, and a lot of people owned airplanes. There were Army surplus airplanes everywhere. Everybody was enthused about it. Eventually, it died away. It was a hobby that came and went, but it sure was fun."

When Russell wasn't flying, he was selling farm machinery from a building at the airport. In 1946, Russell ran for Mayor of Springfield on the suggestion of a friend who didn't like the incumbent. To his own surprise, Russell won the election. After serving a two-year term as mayor, he was elected to the City Council, and played a big part in getting improved electric service installed in Springfield. Russell also served on the school board, but left politics altogether in the early 1950s to start a trucking business and propane gas dealership. He gradually got out of flying and (in 1963, after being divorced) started a new business as an irrigation well contractor. Russell remarried in 1973, but stayed in Springfield. He is still working in the well and pump business, but has been "trying" to retire for several years.

Early in 1991, with the help of Rick School, Robinson embarked on a paper chase which lasted almost two years while he tried to persuade the Government to verify his eligibility for the Purple Heart. After writing many letters to various agencies and records centers, Russell finally received his decoration in November of 1992.

Tom Sowell was also able to return to combat after six weeks. Sowell became a tail gunner and rejoined the 351st on some of the missions to the German rocket bases at Peenemunde: "After my leg was healed, I had to prove to the flight surgeon that I could stand up to (fire a gun). He made me crawl around the airplane and fire from different gun positions. The tail gun position had a seat like a bicycle, or a tractor. It was metal, and you sat astride of it. It was pretty comfortable. I flew back there on three missions over Peenemunde, where the Germans made those missiles, the V1s and V2s. Once when we were flying, I saw them launch a V2. I was supposed to take movies of the mission, so

Post Mission, Post War

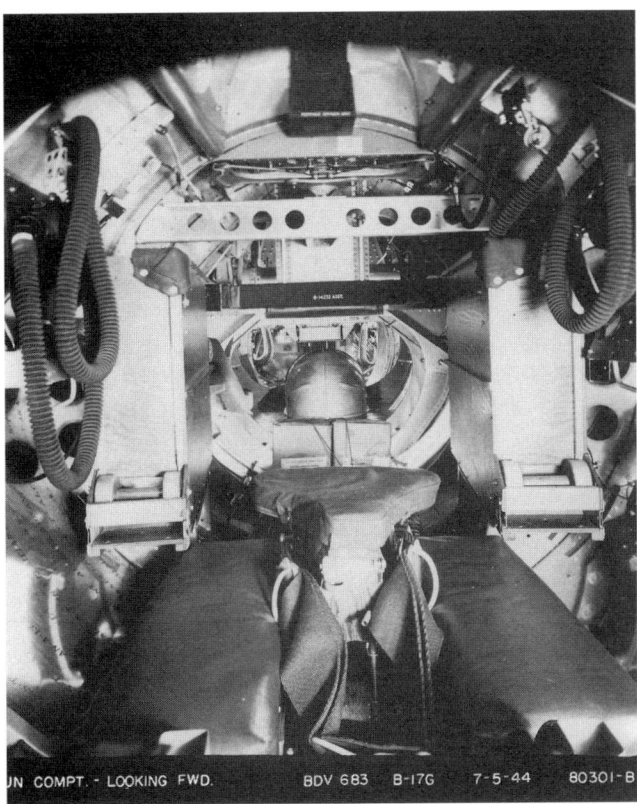

A view looking forward through the tail gunner's position. Note the bicycle type seat and the pads for the gunner to kneel upon. The round object in the center of the photo is the cover for the tail wheel well. (The Boeing Company Archives)

I rolled the camera and got film of one of those rockets coming right up at us. It was coming up in a big circle. It kept circling as it climbed, and went above us by about ten thousand feet, still flying in a circle. I hoped it wouldn't come down and hit us.

"I saw what those things could do on the ground. Once when I was visiting an English girl at her parent's house, a buzz bomb came overhead. We were sitting at a big oak table, and we got under it for cover. That bomb landed nearby and exploded. Broken glass and wood splinters showered down around us. I got cut on the thumb, but that English girl was more seriously hurt. The house was hit pretty bad, too. The slate roof tiles were blown off, all of the windows were broken, and the heavy main stairway collapsed."

Tom Sowell flew more than twenty missions. He saw frequent action, and was credited with a split victory for helping to shoot down an Me163 rocket fighter. Even so, Sgt. Sowell was always glad to get back on the ground: "Flying tail gunner was ok, but I didn't like to fly combat. To tell you the truth, I was scared every time I crawled into the tail of a B-17. You show me the guy who says he wasn't scared, and I'll show you a liar."

Tom Sowell returned to duty as a tailgunner.

Like Russell Robinson, Tom Sowell didn't receive his Purple Heart right away. As it turned out, this worked to his advantage: "I came home before the war ended. My mother received a telegram

Valor at Polebrook

The surviving Ten Horsepower crewmen flew many more missions during the spring and summer of 1944. This photo shows a B-17G of the 511th Squadron at the moment of truth. The white streaks are from smoke canisters dropped by pathfinder aircraft to mark the target.

saying I had been wounded in action. That telegram was from the war department, and somehow, it got back to my personnel file. We got points for our combat service, and if you had 100 points, you could get out. I got credit for being wounded in action, and that gave me enough points to go home. Then they gave me the Purple Heart. There wasn't any ceremony, but I was on my way home."

Tom Sowell left the Air Force to take a Civil Service job. It wasn't long before flying seemed very attractive again: "I had a white collar job. It was paying two-thousand and twenty dollars a year. I found out that if I never went any higher on the pay scale, I'd only get fifty-four dollars a month retirement after twenty years. And I said, 'Holy heck, I'm going back into the Air Force. I can retire as a private in the Air Force and get ninety dollars a month.' So I told my boss I wanted my pay totaled out, and then I quit. And he said, 'Tom, you can't quit.' And I said, 'I just did.' That was in October of 1947."

Tom Sowell stayed in the Air Force for seventeen more years, working as a mechanic on B-17s, B-25s, B-29s, C-54s, and B-52s. He served as an inspector and a maintenance instructor later in his career. Sowell and his family spent much of his service life in Little Rock, Arkansas, with brief deployments overseas. He retired from the Air Force in 1964, and returned to a Civil Service job in New Boston, Texas. Sowell worked as an ammunition/ordnance inspector and automotive maintenance quality control officer until his retirement in 1975.

Post Mission, Post War

Mac Hagbo was not injured while bailing out of Ten Horsepower, and was able to resume flying duties after a brief rest period. Hagbo survived the war, and returned to the Seattle area to manage a hotel. Tom Sowell kept in touch with his wartime buddy, and visited him in 1951. Sowell says that little had changed between them: "Mac's dad still worked as a longshoreman. He'd come in every afternoon with his pockets bulging with jumbo Japanese frog legs. Mac's wife would make up the frog legs, and salmon, and home fried potatoes, and Mac would go under the bar and bring up the beer. I stayed up there three days, and on the last day we had quite a few empty beer cases sitting at the bar." Tom Sowell has many good memories of Mac Hagbo, who passed away in 1969.

Rex, Robinson, and Sowell make special mention of Carl Moore. Each man acknowledges that if Carl had not pulled the plane out of the spiral, none of them would have survived. Carl Moore was awarded the Distinguished Service Cross for bringing Ten Horsepower under control, and for helping to fly the plane after the pilots were disabled. Sgt. Moore returned to combat as a replacement crewman, and flew on many of the spring and summer raids despite his ongoing battles with airsickness. As Moore was nearing his twenty-fifth mission, the total required before rotating home was raised to thirty. Carl kept flying, hoping to reach the magic number, but again the total was increased by five. Sgt. Moore managed to fly number thirty-five before the Air Force could change its mind a third time.

Mac Hagbo outside of his tail gun position.

Russell Robinson and Carl Moore proudly display the 510th Squadron patch on their leather flying jackets.

Carl came home in October of 1944 and married Ellen Garrison, his sweetheart from before the war. The whole town of Williamsport, Pennsylvania turned out to greet their hero, and to congratulate the newlyweds. After their honeymoon, Carl

Valor at Polebrook

The temporary graves at Cambridge Military Cemetery.

Sergeant Carl Moore, in dress uniform, displays his Distinguished Service Cross, Spring, 1944.

and Ellen moved to Langley Field, Moore's first Stateside assignment. Staff Sergeant Moore stayed in the Air Force until 1950, then decided to return to Williamsport. He took a job with an automotive dealership, and was ultimately promoted to Service Department manager.

After Ellen, Carl's second love was singing. He was soon back in place as tenor soloist with several local choirs. He also became a Cub Scout Pack leader. Church and community were always important to Carl Moore. His many friends were stunned when he succumbed to a heart attack while at work in September of 1966. The fondness people felt toward Carl is evident in his obituary: "Blessed with a magnificent voice, Mr. Moore probably sang in more churches and before more audiences in the last twenty years than any other resident. This he delighted to do, and by being so generous in the use of his talents, he

Post Mission, Post War

enriched the musical appreciation of a generation. In his death, we here make record of his heroism as a defender of our country in days of peril, but what saddens our hearts is the loss of a friend who sang so beautifully, so readily, and so happily."

Lt. Clarence R. Nelson, Flight Officer Ronald Bartley, Lt. Walter E. Truemper, and Sgt. Archibald Mathies were posthumously awarded the Purple Heart. Their bodies were temporarily interred at the military cemetery in Cambridge, England. In late Spring of 1944, at the request of David Mathies, the four adjoining graves were photographed by John Romack, base photographer for the 4th Fighter Group. Eventually, each of the fallen airmen was returned to the United States for final burial.

Lt. Nelson was laid to rest in the National Cemetery at Rock Island, Illinois. Established in 1863 as a burial place for soldiers of the Union Army, the Cemetery now bears the remains of 10,000 U.S. service men and women. Ceremonies honoring the dead are held annually on Veterans Day and Memorial Day, and the immaculately maintained grounds provide a dignified and peaceful atmosphere in which visitors may pay their respects.

Dick Nelson's grave in Rock Island National Cemetery, Illinois.

Valor at Polebrook

Memorial services for Ronald Bartley were held on March 26th, 1944, in the Underwood, North Dakota High School auditorium. Family, friends and relatives filled the hall to pay their respects to Ronald and to console his widow, Bernice. Music and prayer were followed with a eulogy given by the Reverend Kenneth Wiley, pastor of the Lutheran Church of Underwood. Memorial donations were distributed among the Red Cross and other war relief charities. Ronald Bartley was buried in the Custer National Cemetery at the Little Bighorn Battlefield in Montana.

The Truemper family was stunned when confirmation of Walter's death reached them in Aurora. Stories printed immediately after the crash mentioned some of the survivors by name, and though none of the dead fliers had been identified, the Truempers knew the men with whom their boy flew. Inevitably, the telegram from the War Department arrived, followed soon after by a letter from Colonel Romig. With their worst fears confirmed, the grief-stricken family gathered it's courage and prepared to say good-bye to their brother and son.

On March 5th, relatives and friends of Walter Truemper filled St. Paul's Lutheran Church in Aurora to hold a memorial service. From the flower covered alter, Pastor W. G. Stallman delivered the obituary and eulogy, reminded those present of Walter's enduring faith, and assured them that he had entered Eternal Life. After prayers were offered and condolences given, the mourners left the church, each taking their own thoughts of a brave and decent young man who would not soon be forgotten.

Ronald Bartley's grave in the military cemetery at Custer National Battlefield, Montana.

Walter Truemper's grave in St. Paul's Lutheran Cemetery, Aurora, Illinois.

Post Mission, Post War

Mrs. Friedericka Truemper accepts the Medal of Honor on behalf of her son Walter. Walter's father is at left, his sister Ann at right. (Note Walter's Navigator's wings on his mother's blouse.) July 4, 1944.

Walter Truemper's heroism and sacrifice were of such magnitude that the Air Force would not forget him either. On May 15th, 1944, Secretary of War Henry L. Stimson signed President Roosevelt's order which posthumously awarded Lt. Truemper his country's highest decoration, the Medal of Honor. The Medal of Honor was usually presented in Washington DC, but Mrs. Truemper's poor health prevented her from traveling. Upon her request it was agreed that the presentation would be made in Aurora.

On July 4th of that summer, a simple gathering took place on the lawn outside of the Truemper home. Shortly before the ceremony was to begin, Walter's brothers Fred and Carl carried Mrs. Truemper in a rocking chair to a spot beneath a large shade tree. Next to her were her husband, Henry, and her daughter, Ann. With family, friends, and military officials watching, Brigadier General R. E. O'Neal read the citation recalling Walter's selfless actions in trying to save the life of his friend. Then, O'Neal

Valor at Polebrook

bent down and gently lowered the ribbon over Mrs. Truemper's neatly gathered hair. One account of the proceedings states that Mrs. Truemper sobbed openly while the citation was read, but when the medal was in place around her neck, "she wiped her eyes, held her head high, and smiled."

Following the ceremony, Mr. Truemper spoke briefly on behalf of his family. "We are proud of the Air Corps," he said, "and of Walter. Our only regret is that he cannot be here to accept this decoration for himself."

Watching silently among the crowd were Mr. and Mrs. C. Richard Nelson, parents of the man for whom Walter had died. Speaking to reporters, the Nelsons described the friendship they had seen while visiting in Alexandria. "The boys were like brothers," they said.

Following the official activities, Mrs. Truemper went inside and patiently sat for more photographs. From a portrait on the wall behind her, Walter seemed to be watching over his mother. Finally, the last flashbulb popped, the reporters and military people left, and the Truemper family was left alone to mourn their loss.

Walter Truemper's body was returned to Aurora for burial at St. Paul's Lutheran cemetery. In memory of their fellow citizen, the people of Aurora erected a monument to Walter in Phillips Park. Shaped from two colors of grey granite, the obelisk near the park's Victory gardens still stands as a reminder of the sacrifice of the young navigator.

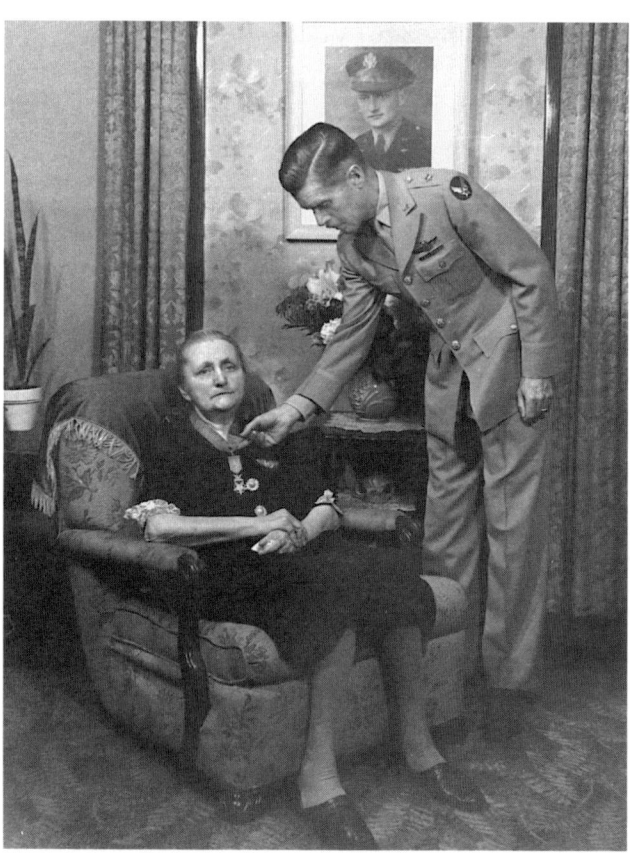

Mrs. Truemper sits for an "Official" Army Air Force photo following the Medal of Honor ceremony. July 4, 1944.

The monument to Walter Truemper in Phillips Park, Aurora, Illinois. The lower inscription states "THIS MONUMENT, ERECTED BY THE CITIZENS OF AURORA, IS GRATEFULLY DEDICATED TO LT. WALTER E. TRUEMPER, USAAC, WHO'S HEROIC SACRIFICE HAS WRITTEN A MOST GLORIOUS PAGE IN AURORA'S HISTORY"

Post Mission, Post War

On October 23, 1983, Building #3750 at Mather AFB, in Sacramento, California was dedicated as "Truemper Hall." Mather was an appropriate choice, as it is the only navigator training base in the USAF. It is easy to see why the Air Force chose to honor Lt. Truemper by naming the training center after him, but it may be difficult for some to understand how the loss of one seemingly ordinary man could touch so many lives. Excerpts from letters written by Ann Truemper Prestero offer a glimpse of what her brother was like, and why he meant so much to those who knew him: "Giving your life for a friend. That's the greatest thing you can do. It takes a strong guy to do that. He was a very caring person. Walter was very active in his church. He went through eight years of parochial school. Prior to his induction into the service, Walter was a leader of the Youth Group of our Lutheran Church. He had a wonderful way with both the young and the old. Truly a very caring young man. I can see that he would not forsake Nels (Lt. Nelson) as long as a breath remained in his body. The two of them were very close friends, and were two of a kind.

"Walter was deeply devoted to our mother. He wrote home daily, because our mother thrived on the little visits via mail. In one of his letters home, Walter explained that they hadn't had any mail for over a month. He was lost without his daily letters in which he was apprised of all the goings on at home. Wally wrote so many interesting things, serious and lighthearted both, about things that transpired on their week ends, and expressions of the friendships that existed among the crew. We received his last letter, dated February 19th, 1944, after we had received the War Department's fatal telegram, which broke our hearts. My mom and dad never got over it before their deaths."

In a letter written for Mother's Day of 1943, Walter told his mother what was most important to him, and prophetically acknowledged the ultimate consequence of war. Ann Truemper Prestero shares part of that letter:

"It takes times like these to show a person how much his mother really means to him.. What this letter is trying to say is that I realize, and have always realized what a wonderful mother I really have. If it were possible for me to be with you, then it would be a simple matter for me to express myself. But as it is, words must suffice.

"I want to thank you for the countless hours you have spent worrying about my welfare, as well as the years spent in raising me from childhood to the man I am today. My life has been such that I would not trade one minute of it for anything worldly. As it has turned out, that you had to raise me in the years foreboding conflict, there is still no regret in my heart. Now, I see my duty to see this war through to a most successful conclusion, so that in the days to come my life can be better for it. When we are together again, God willing, you will realize just how my feelings are towards you.

"If it is my lot to be one of those who suffer the extreme sacrifice, I will be proud to do it if our way of life will continue. It is much better for a man to die for his country and for his God if it is to a successful conclusion so that both the kingdom of God and our country will survive...

Valor at Polebrook

"My reason for saying this is to let you know that it is possible that we may never meet again. If this is the case, I just want you to know that regardless of what happens, it is for the best. I wasn't going to mention this, but I might as well pour out everything in my heart.

"In closing, let me say that I hope you have a most wonderful Mother's day. A day so nice as to be worthy of a mother like you. May our Lord bestow his richest blessing upon you and keep you until the day when we can spend a memorable reunion day together.

With all my love, Mom
Your boy, Walter

Three weeks after the Truemper presentation, a similar scene was played out in Finleyville, Pennsylvania, the home of the Mathies family. Archie Mathies was also awarded the Medal of Honor, and Mrs. Mathies had also requested that the presentation be made in her son's home town. On July 23, family and friends gathered at the First Presbyterian Church in Finleyville to honor the fallen hero. From an alter nearly surrounded with lush, green ferns, Minister Arthur L. South lead the congregation in prayer and song, then offered a reading of Scripture before standing aside to allow the Air Force officers to speak of Archie's bravery and devotion. Major General Howard A. Craig presented the medal to Mary Mathies, who smiled through her tears as he placed the ribbon around her neck. With a heavy heart, Mrs. Mathies also braved the post ceremony photo session. It was the first of several to follow, as more and more people took notice of Archie's sacrifice.

Walter Truemper

The First Presbyterian Church, Finleyville, PA. July 23, 1944. (Photo courtesy of David Mathies.)

Post Mission, Post War

Mrs. Mary Mathies accepts the Medal of Honor on behalf of her son Archie. July 23, 1944. (Photo courtesy of David Mathies.)

This monument, erected by the Pennsylvania Coal Company, honors United Mine Worker's Union members who gave their lives in World War II. The central column is dedicated to Archie Mathies. (The inscription reads ARCHIE MATHIES - STAFF SERGEANT - U.S. ARMY AIR CORPS - BORN JUNE 3, 1918 AT STONEHOUSE, SCOTLAND. - KILLED IN ACTION OVER ENEMY OCCUPIED EUROPE IN THE FLYING FORTRESS "MIZPAH" - FEBRUARY 20, 1944 - GREATER LOVE HATH NO MAN THAN THIS - THAT HE LAY DOWN HIS LIFE FOR HIS FRIEND)

Carl and Ellen Moore with Mary Mathies at the monument to Archie.

On November 19, 1944, Mrs. Mathies dedicated a large stone monument donated by the men with whom Archie worked at the Montour coal mine. The Pennsylvania Coal Company renamed a mine near Finleyville for Archie. A later owner of the Company christened one of its river boats "MV Mathies". (MV is a nautical abbreviation for "motor vessel".)

These civilian honors have been followed by additional recognition from the military. A plaque dedicated to Archie is displayed in Soldiers and Sailors hall in Oakland, California. His portrait hangs in the Hall of Valor at the Air Force Museum in Dayton, Ohio. In 1976, a section of the Airmen's Dormitory at the now decommissioned Chanute Field in

Valor at Polebrook

Illinois was renamed Mathies Hall. In 1977, Mathies Manor, another dormitory, was dedicated at Bolling Air Force Base in Washington, DC, along with dormitories at Perrin AFB in Texas, and Ramstein AFB in Germany. On February 13, 1987, the Mathies NCO Academy was dedicated at RAF Upwood, England. David Mathies spoke on his brother's behalf at some of these later ceremonies.

Of the many monuments which have been erected to preserve the memory of Archie Mathies, the simplest, but perhaps the most significant, is his gravestone in the cemetery at Library, Pennsylvania. (Photo courtesy of David Mathies)

Bombardier Joe Martin's contact with his crewmates ended when he bailed out of Ten Horsepower. Faced with a crisis which threatened all on board, Lt. Martin had only seconds to assess the situation and make the most important decision of his life: "I was manning the nose gun, the turret under the nose of the plane. I saw the fighters coming in, and I was firing at them. The one that hit us came pretty close to crashing into our plane. When we were hit, Lt. Truemper went to see what had happened. I was scared, but I kept firing back, and suddenly everything became quiet. I went back to the cockpit, and to my horror, I found the copilot practically headless, and the pilot badly shot up. I thought they were both dead. The cockpit was a mess. The windshield was shattered, and it was freezing up there. The copilot had fallen into the controls, and we had gone into a dive. I pulled him back and set the plane on automatic pilot. Then I went back up into the nose to get my 'chute, and on the way I tried to open the escape hatch, but it wouldn't move. I called to the crew to prepare to bail out. I opened the bomb bay doors, to give them another way out, and I salvoed the bombs. There was still no sign of anyone alive in the nose. I didn't know where Lt. Truemper had gone. I looked back, and I saw the hatch had opened. It might have been from the draft when I opened the bomb bay doors, but I also thought maybe Lt. Truemper had jumped. I believed I was the last one on the plane, and I bailed out."

Joe Martin could not have known that the intercom and the automatic pilot had been damaged in the attack. Crew members in the aft fuselage reported hearing him give the bail out order, but it is possible that their replies could not be heard in the nose. The 20mm shells which damaged the intercom wiring in the bomb bay also severed some of the control cables routed overhead. These damaged cables may have prevented the auto-pilot from working properly. Sgt. Moore reported that each time it was engaged on the flight home the plane went into a dive, which appears to be what happened when Joe Martin turned on the auto-pilot before he bailed out.

Lt. Martin expected to see other parachutes below him as he descended, but

Post Mission, Post War

found himself alone in the sky: "I couldn't see any one else, no formation, no other planes, nothing. Then a German fighter pilot spotted me and followed me down. I started looking around for the others, but I didn't find anyone.

"I was captured soon after I landed. The Germans moved me around from one place to another, one little jail, one little dungeon. They didn't always feed me, and I damn near froze to death. Sometimes people threw rocks at me. It wasn't fun, I'll tell you.

"I spent the next year in a POW camp, trying to find out what had happened to my crew. I always wondered why none of them ever showed up in camp. After I was liberated and got back to England I learned that they had made it back but the plane had crashed."

Joe Martin stayed in the Air Force until 1946. He was recalled during the Korean Conflict, then left the Service with the rank of Captain. Joe returned to private life, and found success as a businessman, but his thoughts of the mission and his time as a prisoner made it uncomfortable for him to face his former crewmates. He is still haunted by his memories: "I know there were some who thought I shouldn't have jumped. I don't feel bad about bailing out, I just feel bad about bailing out ahead of everybody else. I thought they were already out. Thanks to Lt. Nelson, I knew more about landing that airplane than anybody else left on board. And the rest of them stayed with it. It should have been me and Walter, or me and Archie. I try to forget what happened, but I've prayed for these brave friends every day."

The life-or-death decision faced by Joe Martin and every other flier who bailed out during the war is put into perspective by Lt. Colonel Mark Wells of the U.S. Air Force Academy. In a report entitled AVIATORS IN AIR COMBAT, Wells says the following:

"Some of the worst moments were occasioned by events which took place on board an aircraft immediately after battle damage. Few other situations were as stressful, nor clearly demonstrated a greater impact of chance on an airman's survival. Depending on the extent of damage inflicted during an attack, the occupants of a bomber aircraft might have to react within seconds to save their lives. Some airplanes exploded instantly in balls of fire when hit. Others might be flown straight and level long enough to permit their crews to bail out. While abandoning an airplane, men had to reckon with a multitude of things that could go wrong. Riddled fuselage structures, or weak and burning wings might collapse and send bombers hurtling earthward with terrific centrifugal force, pinning crewmen helplessly inside. Because of their bulk, parachutes were not worn directly, but required attachment before jumping. Moving even a few feet in a burning and wildly gyrating aircraft could be impossible. Hatches on some aircraft were poorly located, difficult to operate, and in at least one case, almost criminally too small for easy egress."

None of the surviving crewmembers feel that Joe Martin was wrong to bail out. Each recalls that in training, Lt. Nelson stated that if the alarm bell rang it would be every man for himself. Joe Rex and Tom Sowell say that they were preparing to jump after the alarm sounded but the plane fell into its spiraling descent before they could put on their parachutes and get out. When questioned by base officers after the mission, Joe, Russ, and Tom each stated that the bail out order had been given, and that Joe Martin did what they were all trying to do. They hold him entirely free of blame.

The crash site on Denton Hill has been a place of wonder for several generations of curiosity seekers, history buffs, and serious aircraft archeologists. For years following the crash, a large mound of dirt was visible at the point where Ten Horsepower first struck the hill. The long, twisting furrows scraped into the hillside by the careening bomber could be seen for several months afterward, but continuous farming of the land eventually smoothed them over. Pieces of metal were frequently turned up by the plowshare. Some bits of wreckage remained lodged in the overhanging treetops for many years before falling back to the ground. Local treasure hunters often walked the slope and the tree line, hoping to find fragments of the plane or some of the hundreds of rounds of machine gun ammunition still on board when the bomber crashed. One such person was Arthur Pettifor, the Observer Corps officer who watched the plane crash from his post on a hilltop in Sawtry. After one day of searching which yielded many incendiary rounds and other pieces from the plane, Mr. Pettifor parked the wagon bearing his finds outside his home in Glatton, only to return to find the entire cache had been stolen.

Interest in the hill was rekindled in 1992 when a local newspaper printed an article about a young American man researching the story of the crash. This man was Rick School. Soon afterward, the hill was overrun by "every yo-yo with a metal detector or shovel within 100 miles," according to Mr. Geoff Farrington, who still actively farms the hill. Until the recent invasion, Mr. Farrington didn't mind the occasional visitor on his property. Angered by the lack of respect shown by many uncaring explorers, he now allows only a select few to go up to the site.

On February 20th, 1994, a small group from the Mathies NCO Academy gathered on the country road below Denton Hill. Although the sun shone down through a cloudless sky, the day was cold and damp. A grey haze hung above the surrounding farm fields and woodlands. Atop the hill, untouched by winter snow, brown-green grasses and leafless trees swayed in the steady breeze which swept across the slope where Ten Horsepower returned to earth for the final time. The ankle-deep stubble left from harvest and the tall grass that had grown in afterward said nothing of the violent impact that once scarred the site.

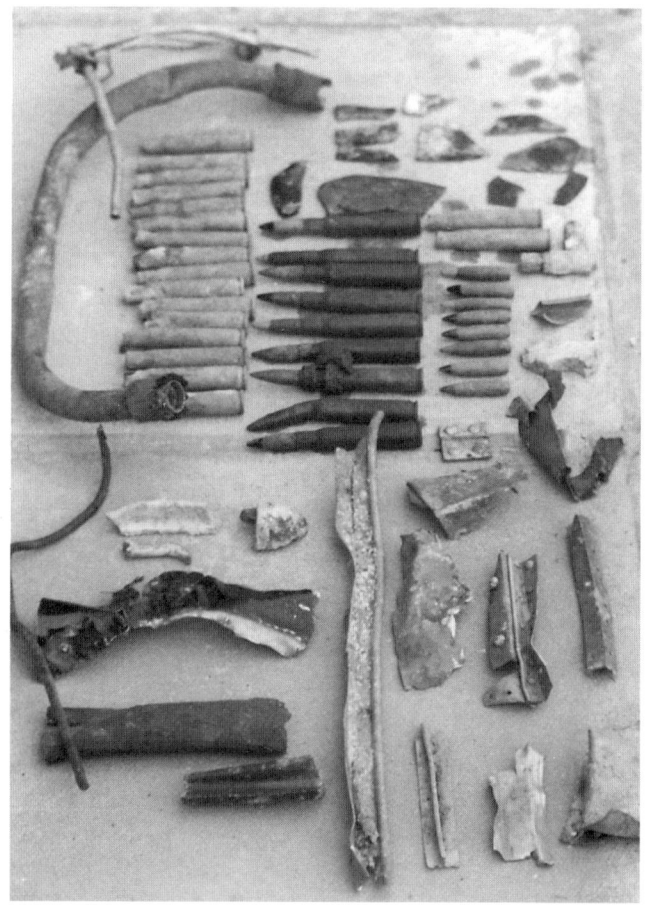

Pieces of the aircraft recovered from Denton Hill.

Post Mission, Post War

Denton Hill, looking southwest across the area where most of the wreckage came to rest, as photographed in Spring of 1992.

The group split up and began a search of the crash path. The metal detector lead them directly up the face of the slope, and when they were finished their artifact bag held several bullets and one other very appropriate find. A curved, triangular piece of metal which had been buried almost one foot below the surface appeared to be a piece of the casting from the ball turret, Archie Mathies' position. It had remained undetected for fifty years.

After reaching the tree line, the group held an informal ceremony beneath the large oak tree at the end of the crash path. A small "altar" was put together, composed of a plaque bearing the date and the aircraft name, a tumbler of scotch for each of the men who died on the flight, two American flags, and a bouquet of flowers. A tape recording of "Amazing Grace", played on bagpipe and organ to recall Archie's Scottish ancestry, provided the background as those present looked down the slope and tried to imagine the scene as the plane approached and hit. They drank a toast to the departed fliers, then began one last ritual before leaving the site. A hole was dug in front of the "altar", into which was placed a bag containing a commemorative coin and program from a banquet

Valor at Polebrook

celebrating the tenth anniversary of the Mathies NCO Academy, in conjunction with the fiftieth anniversary of the crash. The hole was filled, and the two American flags were planted on top, one each for Archie and Walter. As a final honor, the flowers were laid across the surrogate grave.

As the people from the Mathies NCO Academy were leaving, they passed two others who had come to note the passing of the half-century. The first was Mr. David Clark, who has spent many years locating and exploring crash sites of World War II aircraft. In high school, Clark had been recognized as Young Archeologist of the Year for his work with the recovery of artifacts from Ten Horsepower. In many visits to the hill over several years, he has collected a considerable amount of remnants from the plane. The second man was Mr. Andrew Dick, also an aviation enthusiast and archeologist. Andrew knew the hill still contained pieces of the plane, but on that day, he and Mr. Clark did not intend to dig for them. Instead, they climbed to the tree line to reflect on the actions of the men who had died there. Half a mile to the east, traffic hurried up and down the A1 highway. Just out of sight beyond the road, the remnants of Glatton airfield marked the final turning point for Walter Truemper and Archie Mathies. Four miles to the west, some maintenance hangars and a few feet of Polebrook's perimeter track and secondary runways were all that remained of the airfield the brave fliers tried so desperately to reach.

David and Andrew stood in quiet conversation, mutually acknowledging the valor of two unselfish young men. Gradually, the tree shadows grew longer across the eastern slope of Denton Hill, and the wind blew a little bit colder. About the time of day when fifty years earlier a youthful Reginald Griffin had run up the hill to see what had happened, the two historians walked back down knowing the story only too well. They drove off to return to the security of life in peacetime England, and the hill was left to the silence of nightfall.

 # Chapter Eight: Letters

```
ea ba 10  PZ Underwood  N Dak 810 am Mar 3

Mrs Clarence Stadick
11125 Kirk Court
Kirkland Wash

Word Just Received Ronald     Killed in action letter Soon love

                         Dad......840 am
```

Word of the deaths of the four Ten Horsepower crewmen was slow in reaching their next of kin. Newspaper accounts of the mission and the landing attempts appeared in many American newspapers on February 21, but the names of the lost fliers were withheld from the story. Even so, some of the family members recognized the names of the other crewmen, and began to fear the worst. That first news story drew the attention of editors all across the country, and during the next several weeks other newspapers ran duplicates, excerpts, or much altered variations. Parents and siblings of the crewmen depended on these reports, for it was their only link to what was going on, but sometimes the few facts that were known were lost to the zealousness of sensationalizing writers.

Valor at Polebrook

Even before the inevitable telegrams from the War Department arrived at the homes of those killed, wounded, or missing, the families turned to each other for comfort and support, hoping somehow to learn more of what had happened to their boys. Parents and siblings suffered through their grief in an information void. The uncertainty of what had really happened made it all the more difficult to accept their losses. The families knew little more than that their loved ones were gone, or hurt. The letters that began to circulate were the only connection they had to each other, and carried their only hope of finding the answers they so desperately needed. Separated from tragedy by thousands of miles, writing was all they could do.

The following letters have been transcribed from the actual pages written and mailed soon after February 20th, 1944. They have been copied word for word, except as noted. Some of the handwriting was difficult to read, but nothing has been changed, nor the grammar corrected. These letters stand as a testimony of the anguish the family members endured, and of the faith with which they carried on.

From Carl Moore to Mr. And Mrs. Nelson (Dick's parents)

February 26, 1944
England

Dick Nelson between flights at Alexandria, Louisiana, Fall, 1943.

Dear Mr. and Mrs. Nelson,
This is one of the hardest letters I've ever tried to write, but I want to express my deepest sympathy to both of you.
Lt. Nelson was one of the finest men I ever worked with. He kept me going when I was ready to quit because of my constant airsickness. We would all have gladly given our lives to save his, and Archie and Lt. Truemper did that with no questions asked. Your son would have done the same for us
I assure you he did not suffer as I was with him all the time and he was unconscious from the beginning. He and Flight Officer Bartley were struck at the same time. Mac, the tail gunner, and I were the lucky ones of the bunch and we are now on a rest furlough. The other three boys, Rex, Sowell and Robinson have broken legs received in their parachute jumps. They are getting along fine though.
I've almost lost my nerve to keep on but if I can do something to repay the enemy for what they did, I'll be satisfied. I know Lt. Nelson would want it that way.
Mac and I went to the funeral and it was a very nice military one. They are in an American cemetery.
Once again may I express my sympathy to you. I would be very pleased to hear from you at anytime.

Sincerely yours,
Carl Moore

Letters

From Col. Eugene Romig (Polebrook Base Commander) to Mrs. Nelson

February 29, 1944

Dear Mrs. Nelson,

You have been notified that your son, 2nd Lt. Clarence R. Nelson, 0803854, is officially reported as killed in action. I recognize that this announcement causes you greater sorrow than any of us can possibly imagine. We share this feeling with you because he was a good friend and a valuable asset to this organization.

Your son will always be remembered as having set a shining example in the performance of his duty. We will humbly try to do what is required of us remembering his constant devotion to the task which was assigned him. He has contributed his share to the victory which we all desire, and you have made an immeasurable contribution toward that same victory through him.

We want you to know that he will be profoundly missed by his many friends in this organization, nor will the time ever come when he will be forgotten by any of us.

Our prayers are joined with yours during these difficult days.

Respectfully yours,
Eugene A. Romig
Colonel, Air Corps,
Commanding.

From Mrs. Nelson to Mrs. Mathies (The Mothers of Dick and Archie)

March 27th (1944)
3316 Park Ave.
Brookfield, Ill

My Dear Mrs. Mathies,

I have finally recieved all the names and addresses of our crews' parents or relatives. I did so want to write each one and express my love and appreciation for what each member of crew 58 did in trying to bring "Mizpah", our plane, safely to England.

Words fail to express my profoundest love and gratitude to you for the loyalty manifested in Sgt. Archie Mathies. Such loyalty was only surpassed by Christ Jesus, when he too layed down his life for his friends.

Mr. Nelson and I had the extreme pleasure of meeting all the boys last November when we visited the boys in Alexandria. They were a precious group of fine, noble manhood, who were later to prove their mettle.

Sgt. Mathies, Lt. Truemper, Lt. Bartley and our son Dick have made the supreme sacrifice, and my only prayer is that it will not be in vain.

My loving thoughts are with you and yours and should you feel so inclined, would love to hear from you and if you have any clippings would you get some for me? I would greatly appreciate same.

Most lovingly,
Florence E. Nelson

Valor at Polebrook

From Mrs. Mathies to Mrs. Nelson

March 29, 1944
Finleyville, Pa

My Dear Mrs. Nelson,

I was proud to get your letter today. I did hope you would write to me. Well there is not much we can say to each other. We both know the terrible wound it has made in our hearts. Only God alone knows. But I am very proud of Archie. He was not a big fellow, but a big heart, and I am glad that in his last hour he flinched not. He just told me in his very last letter that he had a great love for Dick Nelson, and it has all come out very clearly why he did not bail out. In one of the English papers he said to the control tower he could not bail out for Lt. Nelson was still alive. My other son did not get word about it 'till he saw it in the paper. He at once got permission to go to his brother's base, and by then he was buried. I guess they will all be buried together. My boy told me his Commanding Officer told him the place three miles from Cambridge. I don't think that's very far from London. I have 3 aunts there and they wrote and told me when the good weather comes she is going to the grave. If I had Dick's number when they go I know they would try and find out if they were buried together.

You would get word that they were killed over Glatton, England. I think that should be a lesson to the Army that every one on a plane should have more than either 4 or 8 hours flying time. These two boys I think did a grand job of bringing the plane back.

Did you hear that program on the March of Time when it was broadcast? It said that the two men in the plane, there hands and faces were frozen stiff. There was not a window left in the plane. We will never know their sufferings. Dear Mrs. Nelson, lets remember them as we last saw them. Christ shall clasp the broken chain closed when we meet again.

I will send you this cutting out of our home town paper. Please excuse this writing for it is a mess. I have not been well for a long time myself, low blood pressure, and I think it has put years on me. I guess you'll be the same. Those two cousins that you'll see in the cutting have made their home with me ever since their mother died. I had four of my own, then took them in. I have been all the mother to them as I was to my own, and I dearly love them. My neighbors tell me I should have a seat in Heaven for the Wonderful Mother I have been. I guess that's where Archie got his big heart. Well, Mrs. Nelson, I thank you for your kind words, and if you ever think of having a trip I would be more than happy to have you both come and see us. I am sure we could have a nice time together. I'll close now, and if I get any more news I'll let you know.

Sincerely,
M. Mathies

Sgt. Archie Mathies

Letters

From Mrs. Mathies to Mrs. Nelson

April 13, 1944
Finleyville, Pa

Dear Mrs. Nelson,

Your most kind letter of April 8th gave me a great deal of comfort. I know your heart is broke, just as mine is. I know the wound will never heal. When people gets up over those fifty years its harder to keep the tears away, just like last night in bed. I must of started to dream. I thought I heard myself say, Oh, son, why didn't you bail out. Just in a minute I thought I seen him and he got so mad. And he looked at me and said do you think I would leave Nelson to die alone, and I know well that was his idea, if he could get Dick to Earth. He had told me in one of his letters he was at a Review and seen some of the men and officers get there Medals pinned on them. And he said he was living for the day he would get a few pinned on him. Well, he will, poor kid. I just hope he gets one in the Kingdom of Heaven.

Well I had a letter from Carl Moore in England. He was Archie's pal, and he told me they were all buried together. He had been over to the funeral. I received the Purple Heart Wednesday. I also had a letter from Lt. Martin's mother. He is a prisoner of Germany. You know he bailed out when ever the ship was hit. So he is safe. We'll hope so. It was Archie's sixth mission. He filled a place for a ball turret gunner, the boy was sick that day, for he wrote and told me he was one ahead of his crew.

I don't know any of the rest addresses, only yours and Joe Martin's. Well Mrs. Nelson, I will be glad to hear from you at any time.

P.S. You know Mrs. Nelson I never had Faith of Archie's coming back. I always kept telling the rest of them, now I keep telling myself if I just had that Faith that Martha had. We have always tried to lead a good life and brought up children to both go to Sunday school and Church. My youngest boy he married when only 20 and has a little girl he's never seen. He was sent overseas 6 months before she was born. And they never let him know about Archie. And he seen it in the Paper and at once got leave to go to Archie's base. And I hear that there was not a dry eye in the office when David was there. He kept crying where have you put my brother, where have you put him. His Commanding Officer told him he was buried. They say it took 2 to hold him and give him medicine. He wrote and told me he said, Mom, I'll be a nervous wreck before this is all over. So you see the worries I have before me. And one of the other boys is in Italy on that beachead, on a Tank Destroyer. David and Jim are ground crews. Well, I have to close now hoping to hear from you at a later date.

I remain your sincere friend
M. Mathies

Valor at Polebrook

From Mrs. Nelson to Mrs. Mathies

April 15th, 1944
3316 Park Ave.
Brookfield, Ill

Dear Mrs. Mathies,
I enjoyed your recent letter so much. I have copied the names and addresses of our crew, since you said you didn't have them. I have heard from them all and it is so nice to think we mothers have a bond of affection between us. I know our boys would have liked that. That was an interesting incident, that dream you had. Well, it is true too, those boys all loved one another like brothers and you know they are all safe with God. They are not prisoners of war, maybe to be tortured or have to suffer, and they are not "missing". That suspense would be too terrible. This way their suffering, if there was any, is all over and their earthly "missions are accomplished." Now they are going on to higher ideals with their Heavenly Father because they were all fine, noble, clean moral boys from good homes and parents. So, my dear, we have nothing to worry about. Our boys are safe and happy. Yes, I received a letter from Carl Moore too, telling me all about the funeral and that was comforting to know about it. Have you written your aunt to find out where our boys are buried? If Carl was there maybe sometime he can tell us - when he gets home, but at present censorship forbids. I received a letter from Mrs. Martin too, telling about Joe, but I would rather have it our way, because I have heard of some terrible treatment in the prisoner camps. Try to be as brave as Archie was and pray more to God. We must be good soldiers too, like our dear boys and carry on for those who are left. I find that is the greatest comfort of all, in turning to God in prayer and confidence. We are taught he is loving and kind and moves in "mysterious ways." Thy Kingdom Come, Thy Will Be Done, Not Mine. There is always a reason for whatever He does. So be brave and write when you can.

With all loving
thoughts to you,
Florence E. Nelson

From Mrs. Mathies to Mrs. Nelson

May 3, 1944
Finleyville, Pa

Dear Mrs. Nelson,
I have had such a lot of comfort out of your letters. I keep reading them over again and again. I really like the way you feel about it. Yes its true their Earthly Missions are over and I believe it would be worse if they had been Prisoners of War. I had letters from my other boys in England and they had Carl Moore and Hagbo to see them. David says that Carl Moore seems very broken up over it all, and is inclined to be bitter. He thinks now if he had not lost his head and stayed in the plane with Archie and Truemper he thinks he might of could brought it down to Earth. I feel now that is on that boys mind and he will not get over it. No matter what anyone will tell him, he'll always feel the same.
I sent on some films to England, and I told David and Jim I want some pictures of both Archie's and Dick's grave taken. I feel I would like to have them just to show us where they are laid. That's one comfort in knowing where they are

Letters

buried. Some people will never know what happened to their loved ones. I cut this map out of the paper. I crossed it 3 miles from there. My David says you can get a bus out of Bedford every 2 hours.

Well Mrs. Nelson, you do sound like a good Presbyterian. We are. I will send you this picture of Archie and I taken on his last leave home. My hands are so shaky I can hardly steady them to write so please excuse my writing. Well I have a appointment at the beauty shop. I belong to the Eastern Star, so I have a meeting tomorrow night. I did write to Lt. Truemper's mother, but as yet she has not answered it. Well, Mrs. Nelson, the good weather is beginning to get here. Well I hope this finds you in good health and able to carry on for them that are left. We'll love to hear from you when ever you feel like it.

With best love from
M. Mathies

From Carl Moore to Mrs. Mathies

March 5, 1944
England

Dear Mrs. Mathies,
I hardly know how to write to you but I do want to express my deepest sympathy to you. Archie and I were great pals. He did a great heroic deed in giving his life for his fellow man.

He and I always talked about visiting his aunts, and Mac and I just came back from Glasgow. We saw Mr. and Mrs. Hamilton and also Mrs. Black. Mrs. Bell was not home at the time. I was very glad to meet them. They treated me so very nice.

I have here a picture of you in a gold frame, and one of Thelma and Archie, and Archie himself taken when he was home on his last furlough. David was up to meet me and I was sick with ptomaine poisoning. I didn't get much chance to talk to him. I will see him when I get my next pass. One of the other boys was here to see me while I was on furlough. I'm not sure if it was Jim Scot or not. He said he would be back on his next leave to see me again.

Archie and I talked quite a bit about each others family and girls and I feel as though I know all of you even though we've never met. I would write to Thelma but Archie never told me her address.

I can't think of the right things to say but I just want you to know we are all proud of Archie and all loved him like a brother.

I'll close now and I hope I can hear from you sometimes. Mac and I are going to continue and maybe we can do something to repay for all the grief everyone has been through.

Yours truly,
Carl Moore

Valor at Polebrook

From Carl Moore to Mrs. Mathies

April 3, 1944
England

Dear Mrs. Mathies,

I was afraid something had happened to my letter I had written you but I see you received it alright. It was the best I could do for you to tell you what happened in my own words. Archie was a swell fellow, and as you say, with a heart as big as gold. I sure do miss him, as he and I liked to do about the same things when on leave. The other fellows and I have different ideas as to having a good time, and on leave I usually wind up by myself. Mac Hagbo and I are going to see Dave (David Mathies) when we get our pass on Wednesday.

None of the boxes you sent ever reached Archie. Did you stop shipment on the watches, or were you too late?

I can see that Thelma isn't important, so enough for her.

I'm not married, but am engaged to a wonderful girl at home, and expect to marry her some day. She used to write to Archie, and once when I called her on the phone from Syracuse Archie talked to her too. She said she would like to write to you, so maybe you'll be getting a letter soon from her. When this war is over I sure hope we can both come out and see you all.

Archie had made three trips altogether. We only had two as a crew. He substituted for another ball turret gunner once. Don't tell my mother how many we have had as I never told her and I don't want her to worry. I have five in now. Mac has six in. We are assigned to another pilot that lost his crew and is building a new one around three of us. He has a radio operator left, and a copilot. There never will be a set of commissioned men like we did have.

All of Archie's personal things were sent to you and Dave got some of his other things. Mac and I went over to the funeral. They were all buried in an American cemetery along with seven others and it was a regular military funeral. Mrs. Hamilton said, when I was up at Stonehouse, that she would like to have had him buried up there but she had so much red tape to go through to get him.

Summer weather is about due to break thru over here. One day we have it, then the next it's either rain or snow.

That's about all for this time except to tell you Rus is getting better. His cast will be on two weeks yet. Tom has his removed and Rex is still in the Hospital.

Sincerely yours,
Carl

Tom Sowell, Carl Moore, and Russell Robinson flew as replacement gunners for several other 351st crews.

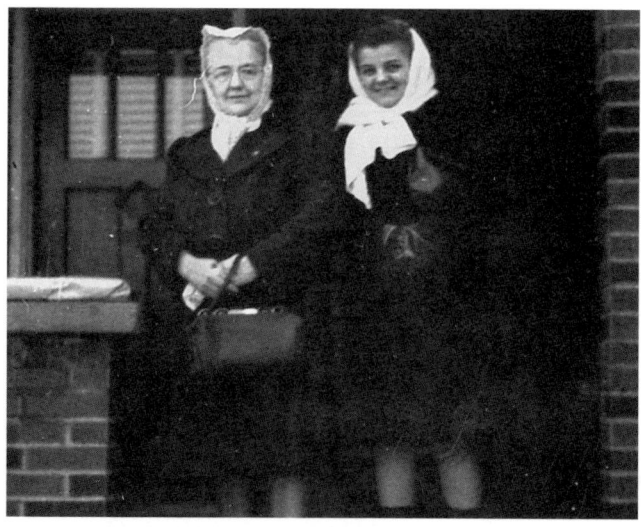

Mary Mathies with Ellen Moore.

Letters

From Louise Rex (Joe's wife during the war) to Mrs. Mathies

Sunday night
March 12, 1944

Dear Mrs. Mathies,

Words don't mean a great deal at a time like this, but I do want to tell you that my heart aches for you and yours. It is doubly hard for me to write this because I feel so grateful to our God for sparing my Joe.

Joe has written many letters since then, (some were very much censored) and has not seemed bitter about losing such dear friends, but very, very sad. He has an arm badly shot up (by the Germans) and a broken leg from the landing, but he seems to be coming along well. He said "Please write to Mrs. Mathies and tell her that I want to come to see her when I come back, God willing. I ask continually why it had to be, for Archie was one of the best buddies I've ever had. He had more intestinal fortitude than any man I've ever known. I wish I could tell him, somehow, how very much we owe to him."

When I wrote before that Joe said they had all taken a turn for the better, I only meant they had all sobered down, and seemed to take it more seriously.

No, we have no children, for Joe and I were only married in September when they had that short furlough, so you can see I haven't had much of a married life yet. But I do love him dearly, and perhaps he has been spared for a purpose.

I know how your heart aches, for I lost my mother and my older sister when I was very young (12) and for a while I was bitter, but God knows best. Please write when you feel able.

In sympathy,
Louise Rex

From Ann Truemper (Walter's sister) to Mrs. Mathies

May 7, 1944
Aurora, Ill.

Dear Mrs. Mathies,

We're so very glad that you wrote to us Mrs. Mathies, as we've been thinking so much of you folks, but never had your address.

It's so very hard for us to express our feelings to you, but you know our feelings and thoughts, as we both have the same wound which must be healed. It seems though as if it will never be healed as the wound is so very deep. But, the Lord wanted it this way, and we will meet on those beautiful shores, and all of this will then be forgotten and we will rejoice with our Wallie and Archie.

You mentioned it was Archie's 6th mission. As far as we know, it was but Wallie's 2nd. I think some of the boys had more missions to their credit than the others.

Mrs. Mathies, have you also tried to visualize the strain and anxiety these two loved ones of ours went through in those hours before their death? I can just picture how Wallie looked, with that very serious and tired look on his face, praying that God would help them land their ship so they could save Dick, their "skipper". They all thought so much of him, and the friendship which existed between them was so very great. They just couldn't leave a friend, still breathing, in the plane. It

Valor at Polebrook

Walter Truemper

wasn't like our boys to do those things, was it? I can only feel that if our Father really wanted them to live and go thru these horrible missions, he would have let them land the plane. They are thru with all of this suffering and strain and can rejoice with our Heavenly Father.

We also have three other boys in the Service, so we have very much in common, haven't we? We must carry on for these, as difficult as it may seem now.

I'm Wallie's sister, Ann, Mrs. Mathies. I'm writing this letter for my wonderful Mother, who has been a helpless invalid for the past ten years. Wallie and I were the two who always took care of Mom when he was home, and it's going to be so very difficult to not have him return when this horrible war is over.

Wallie is just two years older than I, and we were the best of pals. We went everywhere together and we confided in each other always. I never missed writing to Walter each night and sometimes wrote twice. I just can't get used to writing one less, and I sit and think each night of what I might have said and just give up with a lump in my throat. I realize now, more than ever, how very close we were. I'll never forget him.

My Mom is taking this entire tragedy as bravely as anyone possibly could. She's also so very broken-hearted, but knows she must carry on for her other three, but she feels now that she has something to look forward to when meeting her Wallie.

I will close for now, Mrs. Mathies, and hope and pray that God will give us all the strength and courage to carry on as our Wallie and Archie would want us to. We will be looking for another letter from you.

Very Sincerely,
Mrs. Truemper and Ann

P.S. Will be wonderful to receive a picture of Archie's grave, as you said. I know how Mom would like one of Wallie's, too.

Letters

From Mrs. Helen Martin (Joe Martin's Mother) to Mrs. Nelson

March 1, 1944

Dear Mrs. Nelson,

I am the mother of Joseph Martin, who was the bombardier of the plane crew on which your son is pilot. Today I received a telegram saying Joe has been missing from Feb. 20th. I was wondering whether you had any word from your son that could give me any information at all about Joe. I would be very thankful. All I know is that he was over Germany.

I am enclosing a stamped, self-addressed envelope for your answer.

Anxiously awaiting your reply, I am

Sincerely,
Mrs. John Martin
637 Bordentown Rd.
Burlington, N.J.

From Mrs. Martin to Mrs. Nelson

March 11, 1944
637 Bordentown Rd
Burlington, New Jers

Dear Mrs. Nelson,

I'm sorry that I haven't answered your letter earlier, but we have been waiting to hear from all the families of the crew hoping to get some more news of Joe. We have had answers from all now and there's never a word about the bombadier.

The co-pilot, navigator and chief engineer are gone and the other 5 bailed out, each one being hurt. They are at base hospitals in England and although they have written home they did not mention the bombadier either.

I want you to now how truly sorry we are to know that your son was killed on that trip. You have our deepest sympathy Mrs. Nelson.

Joe wrote us about the lovely time he had when you were so very kind to them and I want to say thanks for taking care of him as your own boy. We have had clippings from several papers telling how the Chief Engineer tried to bring in the plane only to have it explode and each time the line is included about "censorship prevents news of the bombardier."

If we hear anything at all I shall write you about it. Again, let me express our regrets for you and yours in your sorrow.

Sincerely,
Helen Martin

(At the bottom of this letter, Mr. Nelson wrote the following note: "Tell Mrs. Martin, Wally and Mathies both brought the plane back - Wally deserves a lot of credit. Dad.")

Valor at Polebrook

From Mrs. Martin to Mrs. Nelson

Late March, 1944

Dear Mrs. Nelson,
Enclosed are the clippings I spoke of and also a copy of the letter Carl Moore sent us as well as the home addresses of the entire crew. I'm sure the folks would appreciate hearing from you too.

The only news of Joe is in the letter and clippings and were hoping and praying for more news of him soon. The Inquirer one you have seen is best.

Sincerely,
Helen Martin

From Carl Moore to Mrs. Martin

March 5, 1944
England

Dear Martins,
Although I have never met you I feel as though I know you. Our crew lived close together since we were organized and we knew quite a bit about each others private life.

When we were hit Lt. Martin bailed out and his chute opened immediately and he was getting along fine the last we saw him. He was not injured and he should be able to work his way back as many others have done.

Only Carl Moore is missing from this photo taken by Archie Mathies outside the crew's barracks in Alexandria. Oct. 28, 1943.

Letters

There is five of us left. Lt. Truemper and Archie Mathies were killed when they attempted to bring the ship down with Lt. Nelson who was unconscious. The rest of us bailed out over the field. Sgts. Rex, Robinson and Sowell broke their legs in the jump. Sgt. Hagbo and I were lucky to come out O.K.

The boys with the broken legs are doing fine. Sgt. Rex was shot in the right arm and was the worse of all. He has been sent to a General Hospital. The other two are walking in casts here in the barracks.

Sgt. Hagbo and I were given a seven day rest furlough and we just came back from Glasgow. We are now ready to go back and try it again.

I hope you get some relief out of this news as I imagine you have only received the Governments cold "missing in action."

I would be glad to hear from you at any time, until then I'll be waiting to receive your letter.

Sincerely yours,
Carl Moore

From Mrs. Martin to Mrs. Nelson

April 5, 1944

Dear Mrs. Nelson,
Am writing you a few lines to let you know that we received a telegram from the War Dept. through the international Red Cross Tuesday April 4th that our son Joe is a prisoner in Germany. We feel you are anxious to know what Joe's fate was knowing what happened to the rest of the crew. While it has eased our minds to know Joe is at least alive, I know how terrible you feel over your Dick's loss and I know God will give you strength to bear up.

Sincerely,
Mrs. John Martin

From Carrie Robinson (Russell's Mother) to Mrs. Nelson

April 2nd, 1944
Springfield, Colo.

Dear Mrs. Nelson,
I am very pleased that you have written to me concerning our boys overseas. I didn't meet any of the crew, but when Russell was home on furlough last September, I asked him about the boys and particularly about his pilot. He spoke very highly of each of them and how well they worked together. He told me he had every confidence in his pilot and the very highest respect for him, not only as a pilot but as a man. Russell said all of the boys felt the same way.

Yes indeed it is too bad it had to happen, but I am thankful they were back in England, not only for Russell's sake, but for the boys who were taken.

We have no idea what Russell will do, but I suppose they will make up another crew. This was their second mission, so he has a long way to go before he is through.

Thank you for writing, and please accept our deepest sympathy.

Sincerely,
Carrie M. Robinson

Valor at Polebrook

From Vera Sowell (Tom Sowell's Mother) to Mrs. Nelson

April 4, 1944
New Boston, Texas

Dear Mrs. Nelson,

There is no words in which to describe the feeling we have for you and yours. It was very much of a shock to us when we received word from the War Department saying that our son was wounded and we send our deepest regrets to the family of Lt. Nelson.

Our son was always telling us what a grand and brave person your son was, and he often said that he was one of the grandest persons he knew.

Richard also spoke about you and your husband visiting them and what a grand time they had.

There is nothing we can do, but hope and pray that this will all soon be over and bring our boys back home.

With loving thoughts,
Mrs. Vera Sowell

From Bernice Bartley (Ronald Bartley's widow) to Mrs. Nelson

Ronald Bartley, while stationed in North Africa.

April 11, 1944
Underwood, N. Dak

Dear Mrs. Nelson,

Was so very glad to receive your letter. There is so very little I can say, but am beginning to realize that God had "other plans" for our boys, and we must do our very best and carry on until we meet again.

Am enclosing a clipping from the Oakland Tribune as I read it on February 21. I was in California at the time. It is needless to say that for the next ten days I prayed that Sgt. Moore had been transferred to another crew (as so often happens). But then my message came! I then realized that I was only trying to push the burden on some other soul, who probably couldn't have shouldered it, as the Lord has given me strength to do.

I am very sorry that I didn't get to meet you folks while you were in Alexandria, but perhaps we shall someday. I too, would like to write to the families of our boys, but have only the addresses of Mrs. Martin, and Mrs. Russell Robinson. Would you be so kind as to send me the others? Would appreciate it deeply.

Thinking of you as Dick's mother, I am,

Sincerely yours,
Bernice Bartley

Letters

From Mrs. Eva Rex (Joe Rex's Mother) to Mrs. Nelson

April 13, 1944
Defiance, Ohio

Dear Mrs. Nelson,

Little did I think when I received your letter that it would be so long before I replied. I did have a letter begun once before, but was interrupted and just couldn't seem to get back to it.

I wanted to write you and the other Mothers as soon as we had word regarding Joe from the War Department. Unfortunately for me, Joe must have forgotten he promised to send me the names and addresses of all mothers of the crew.

Joe had told us what section the boys were from, and had added "Lt. Nelson, our pilot, is from Brookfield, Ill." Telling that I suppose, because his older sister lives in Villa Park.

I have a neighbor who gets a Chicago paper, so I asked her to watch for word concerning your son, and just the day before I received your letter, she brought me the paper with pictures of your son and Lt. Truemper, and the addresses.

It is so difficult to find words with which to express to you the sympathy my husband and I would like to express to you and Mr. Nelson, and the other parents whose sons were members of crew 58, and who like you had to see them sacrificed in this terrible war.

We parents all realize when our boys go into training and then into combat, that they won't all come home but being human we all hope and pray that our sons and their especial buddies may come back. It is in this as in all other instances when death takes a loved one we ask ourselves why one is taken and another left. That is a question only God can answer, and he alone can bring a bit of peace and comfort aye and even later a bit of joy, to the hearts of the stricken.

As my thoughts return again and yet again to the tragic ending of this fine bunch of boys, I continually breath a prayer to God above that he will bring some bit of peace and comfort to all those whose hopes were so quickly crushed. It seems almost a sacrilege for me to thank our Heavenly Father for our Joe's safety when I think of those buddies of his who made the supreme sacrifice.

I know how Joe felt toward each one of the other nine boys and I know to him it is even as though brothers had been taken. To you, Mr. and Mrs. Nelson, I must say that he so often wrote of your son and during the few days he was home, spoke so many times in admiration of "my pilot." And I know that whatever physical suffering Joe may have had to endure, it cannot be compared to the anguish of mind as the days go by and the truth of all this comes home to him.

We have heard from Joe fairly regular, just short V-mail letters, more I am sure to bring us assurance that he is alright. He is just beginning in the last few letters to speak of "that day." We have not plied him with questions, feeling that he will tell us what he can as he can bring himself to speak of it.

We did not know for some time what Joe's wounds were, then little by little we began to get information. Now we know he was wounded in the right arm and hand when a shell exploded in front of him and that later as he bailed out he broke an ankle.

A letter this week says that he has left the wheel chair for crutches but that the doctor informed him it would be June before he could get back to the base. He has said a couple times he was afraid his flying days were over and a nephew (stationed in London as photographer for LIFE and Time magazines) wrote us he

Valor at Polebrook

didn't think Joe would ever fly again. He also said that Joe's gun was literally shot from under him.

Mail was just beginning to get through to Joe when this happened, and with the change in address of course his mail just didn't reach him and he's spent several weeks without any and that began to show in the short notes we had, but just this week came a letter saying he received fifty letters at one time.

I have two letters from Mrs. Martin. The first, asking if we had received any word from our Joe, as they had had only the "Missing in Action" from the War Dept. Then this week the second saying word had come that their Joe was a prisoner in Germany.

But I must bring this to a close. I am sorry to have been so long but rest assured, dear friends, it isn't that I haven't thought of you. Many times a day I ask our Heavenly Father to bring comfort to all parents so afflicted in all this time and a special prayer for you parents of crew 58. Time is a great healer for all troubled hearts and I hope you'll find it so.

I will be so glad to hear from you at any time.

Sincerely your friend,
Eva E. Rex

From Mrs. Howard Moore (Carl Moore's Mother) to Mrs. Nelson

April 14, 1944
Williamsport, Pa

Dear Mrs. Nelson,

I sure was glad to hear from you. It seems as if I knew you folks by hearing from Carl. I had such a nice letter from Mrs. Martin, telling me she had a letter from the government telling her Joseph is a prisoner in Germany, and that was bad enough but at least she knew he was still living.

Carl had such a nice time with you people when you were together. He wrote and told me about it, and about two weeks before (Lt. Nelson) was killed, Carl sent me your address and told me to write to you folks, but I just didn't get to it. Mrs. Nelson, will you send me the other boys' parent's addresses? I have Mrs. Martin's, but not the rest of them.

God seems as if He wants the best of what we have. When I go to bed at night, I pray to him to take good care of my boy, and always be by his side. He sure was with him once, Mrs. Nelson. Carl is such a good Christian boy. He is so good to us.

Mrs. Nelson, don't cry when you read this, but I can hear your boy's voice yet. When they bid me good bye, he said he hoped to meet me face to face when the war is over. I will meet him face to face in Heaven some day. Carl was saying good bye, and he said, "Mother, I want you to meet my pilot."

I don't hear so often from Carl now, as it takes from 18 to 19 days to get letters to us. The hold up is New York City. Well, I have to close now, as I have some more letters to write. When you write to Carl, tell him I wrote to you. He has been asking me if I did. I hope to hear from you again. Carl's address is just the same, only the A.P.O. is 557 instead of 634.

Most Lovingly,
Mrs. Howard Moore
Carl's Mother

Letters

From Louise Rex (Joe Rex's wife during the war) to Mrs. Nelson

April 23, 1944
Richmond, Calif.

Dear Mrs. Nelson,

I have wanted to write you, but I had no address. I've asked Joe to get yours and the others but he didn't get any mail for such a long while and hadn't seen Carl for a month when my request did reach him, as I still haven't received them.

Could you possibly send me Bernice Bartley's address? Is she still in California?

In Alexandria, I got to know most of the boys on "58" and Lt. Nelson, too. I best remember one night we all went to church together and went out to eat oysters afterward. They were all such good pals, and I especially admired your son after the way I have known some officers to act. Some infantry units had a tank on exhibition across the street, and as Lt. Nelson outranked the noncom watching it, he gleefully clambered all over it, and started the engine and the siren. I'll never forget how interested and gleeful he was that night.

Joe has been very lucky, and I'm so very, very grateful that he was spared. I know it has changed him from pretty much of a boy into a man, though. We're both just 22, you know, and Joe and I've been married about eight months, now. So you can see I've not had him long.

Please do let me have Bernice's address if you have it. Perhaps I could see her, as my sister and I leave very shortly for San Fransisco to work, if we like it. We have so many friends and relatives there, and as long as my life is upset, it doesn't matter much where I live, at present.

There's not much to say at a time like this, but to keep you in my prayers, that God may comfort you. You see, it isn't so awfully long since I lost my mother and then my sister, and I know words don't help much. I'm so glad you wrote.

Sincerely,
Louise Rex

From Joe Rex to His Parents (Excerpts from a V-MAIL letter)

May 8, 1944
England

...I have been trying to write to Nels mother for over a week but I have not been able to. It is expecially hard to think about Dick because of all the boys who are gone. He was my ideal. I always used to think back in phase training, "Why can't I be like him?" I have never seen anyone who did not like him nor have I ever flown with a better pilot. We have had a lot of close ones but always Nels knew what to do and did it at the right time...

...Wish if you can tell me anything about Joe, you would. That is the only way we can find out. I am still hoping to be out by July 1st, but can't be sure. Tell Doc Wilson it was a tri moblar fracture...

Love,
Joe

Valor at Polebrook

From Ann Truemper (Walter's sister) to Mr. And Mrs. Nelson

March 21, 1944
Aurora, Illinois

Dear Mr. and Mrs. Nelson,
Yes, it's Ann writing to let you know we were successful in securing our copies from the Philadelphia press. We hope this clipping will mean as much to you as ours does to us.
Remember, Mr. Nelson, you said we should send you a picture of Wallie? Well, we will too! We haven't found the negative so intend to have several copies made from our print. We do want you to have one so you can have it with Dick's. We will wait for one of his snapshots too! They seem to belong together, don't they?
We miss our boy's letters so. He wrote so faithfully that it's so difficult to stop receiving them. He and I were so very close and I guess that accounts for the fact that I can't get used to the idea of not writing anymore. I never missed writing him one day.
I can't write anymore now. I can't talk about it yet and imagine you feel as we do. We did so enjoy your visit, and you were everything Wallie told us you were, and you know what he thought of his "Mom and Dad Nelson".
Our boys are together, enjoying the Peace we now long for. They'll be waiting together for us when we join them.

Yours very sincerely,
Wallie's family
(Mom, Dad, and Ann)

From Carl Moore to Mr. and Mrs. Nelson

April 18, 1944
England

Dear Mr. and Mrs. Nelson,
The last time I wrote to you I forgot to tell you about Dick's personel things. They sent all he had to you. Maybe you have them by now. They collect them right away and turn the other things into the supply room.
I was glad to hear from you and also glad to hear mother has written you.
Mac and I went to the funeral with the Chaplin and his assistant. They buried ten other soldiers along with our boys. Each boy was represented by his respective Chaplin. There were about fifty visitors and about twelve Chaplins there. We all marched out in military order with a color guard ahead of us who shot the gun salute. Each casket was covered with an American flag. Each Chaplin spoke a verse for his boy. It is an American cemetery where they were buried and a very nice place. That's about all there is to tell. I don't remember what the Chaplin said but I imagine you could write to him and he'd be glad to tell you.
I'm glad you are feeling a little better. It is a terrible thing to try and believe but we will try to take their place.
Tom and Russell have both had their casts removed and are getting along fine. Rex is still in a hospital and slowly but surely getting better. We'd like to see him but they move him about every time we get a pass.

Letters

I was sent to London last Tuesday to receive the DSC. General Spaatz presented it. I was sure excited.

That's all for now. Write again soon.

As ever,
Carl

From Carl Moore to Mrs. Nelson

April 25, 1944
England

Dear Mrs. Nelson,

I was afraid my letter hadn't reached you after all but I see it did. I'm so glad it helped to ease your mind.

The clippings from the Inquirer haven't reached me yet. Mother is sending them to me. I had quite a long talk with the correspondent from the Inquirer and I imagine he had a complete story.

All of us always talked about the 4th of July party you had planned, remember? We are having our jackets painted with Mizpah and a picture of a B-17 on our backs. Lt. Nelson had made arrangements the day before the raid and we are having them done anyway. Write to my mother and ask her for a copy of the poem Mizpah I sent her. She is going to write to you and I imagine you'll hear from her before this letter arrives.

Joe Rex is still in the hospital. Here is his address. He'd sure be glad to hear from you. Here are addresses for the parents of the boys who are still here with me.

The prayers of all you at home must surely have saved the rest of us and brought us back. Mac and I have started flying again. We heard today the four of us will be put on a crew with a pilot that lost his last December. There never will be another group of officers like we had. I've flown with quite a few others since then and I can't get to like them as we all did our own men. Never another pilot like Dick. When we were on our first raid we had an instructor pilot with us and while Dick had his radio tuned to other business the instructor said to the rest of us over the interphone, "I want to tell you boys, you have one of the best pilots in the business and I want you to give him your best." We sure tried. He always had big ideas for us.

You are really brave to take this as you have. I only hope I can meet you again soon. They've added five more raids on our 25 now.

I'll close now hoping to hear again from you soon.

I remain one of your boys,
Carl

Mac Hagbo and Russell Robinson model the leather flying jackets they had painted after the crash. The men chose to retain the Mizpah design in memory of their friends.

Valor at Polebrook

From Ann Truemper (Walter's sister) to Mr. and Mrs. Nelson

May 1, 1944
Aurora, Illinois

Dear Mr. and Mrs. Nelson,

When writing the above, I thought to myself what our Wallie would have said, "Dear Mom and Dad!"

Seems strange when one hears the saying now that time heals everything. You know, to me it seems that now more than ever the realization of their being away is felt more deeply than ever. I now know that it is a fact, and will always be so. The 20th will never be forgotten. Was surprised to hear that so many things in your family fall around that date.

You mentioned what a comfort our bonds of friendship hold. Yes, I'm sure Wally and Dick would want it this way. Talking about friendship Mrs. Nelson, we got a wonderful letter today from a friend of Wallie's over in England who is also a Navigator. He was in a station hospital in England when he learned of the tragic news. He was wounded on one of his missions over France. He said that the passing of boys like ours serves to give renewed strength and courage to those who must fight for our quick return to peace. His name was Lt. Williams, possibly the "Skipper" was acquainted with him also. It seems as if these friendships acquired between our servicemen is so much deeper than those in civilian life.

We received a wonderful letter from Sgt. Mathies' mother, and I'm surely going to answer her at once. It was a shame that her other boys were so close and knew of it so late.

You asked if we received any further information from Washington. We received the Purple Heart also, together with the certificate accompanying it. We've also received his six months' gratuity, but none of his personal belongings. Have you heard anything about Dick's clothes, etc? Perhaps it will take a while yet, but we've been wondering if maybe you've had some word regarding it.

Mrs. Nelson, Mom told me to ask you if you thought it might be possible for us in some way to get a connection with someone over there and have some type of wreath, or the like, put on our Wally and Dick's graves for Memorial Day. If it were possible, don't you think it would be nice? Were they here by us, we would give them so many beautiful flowers. If you think it would be possible, would you give us your ideas so we could work something out? We really wouldn't have too much time. Maybe it would be the Chaplain, or maybe Carl Moore, or someone else, but surely someone would be able to find out the location. If it would be permissible, it would be the least we could do, don't you think?

I think I've taken up enough of your time with all my questions, but it seems so easy to talk with you about these things. We hope to hear that you and Mr. Nelson will find time soon to come and pay us another visit. We'll be looking forward to seeing you both. Then, we can talk, and talk, and really learn more about our boys.

Very sincerely,
Mom and Ann Truemper

Letters

From Ann Truemper (Walter's sister) to Mrs. Nelson

May 20, 1944
Aurora, Illinois

Dear Mrs. Nelson,

Just wanted to let you know how much we thought of our Wallie, your Dick and you folks today. It's hard to believe it even tho 3 months have already passed, isn't it? I don't think it will ever get any lighter as time goes by.

I do hope that Carl received my letter in time and that he will be able to take care of the wreath for us. I hope that both our boys are lying side by side and I can't help but believe that they buried all four together. It only seems like the right thing to do. Carl will never be able to realize what he is doing for us, if it is possible for him to do this great favor for us.

I never ever dreamed that this Memorial Day would have such a meaning for us this year. It will seem so very close to home for all of us.

I hope you and Mr. Nelson are fine. Give my regards to Dad when you write, won't you?

With love and sincerity,
Ann

From Jessie Mathies Backstrom (Archie Mathies' sister) to Mrs. Nelson

June 20, 1944
Finleyville, Pa

Dear Mrs. Nelson,

I am Archie's sister, and as my mother is away from home at present I thought I would like to drop you a line.

I had a letter from my brother David, (stationed in England) today and his letter contained some news that I thought you would like to hear.

On Memorial Day he obtained a leave and went to the boy's graves. He said the caretaker took him right to where they were buried. He says he could only get within 30 feet of them, but the four of them are side by side. And the group had sent flowers. We were remarking on Memorial Day that there was no one over there to put a flower on their graves. I am so glad that the Group had not forgotten.

David said it is a beautiful cemetery, but he couldn't take a picture of the graves. He was given a reason for it. But it is a consolation to know that they were all together.

My mother hasn't been too well of late, so maybe a change away from home will do her good. I don't know if she answered your last letter, but thanks a million for writing.

Mrs. Nelson, we think you have been so brave about all this. We have quite a few pictures of Dick, and he was such a handsome boy. Archie thought so much of him. I know it takes great courage on your part to be able not to grieve too deeply. I know Dick must be proud of you now, even as we are proud of them. We are all praying that Peace on Earth, Good will toward Men shall soon come through the bravery of such men!

I will close hoping this finds you well.

Sincerely,
Jessie Mathies Backstrom

Valor at Polebrook

From Joe Rex to Mrs. Nelson

July 12, 1944
England

Dear Mom Nelson,
    Right after my folks visited you, my mom wrote and said you had written to me. I kept waiting and waiting and finally yesterday the letter came. It was postmarked May 20, so I take it it came by canoe or maybe someone swam over with it.
    As you can see by the address I am back with the boys again. It is really nice to be back even though I am grounded. I hope it isn't permanent, but it will be for a long time anyway.
    It is too bad that at least one of us couldn't have kept our 4th of July date in Chicago. You can be sure we all remembered it.
    We thought too that had Joe stayed he could have landed us but what happened will never be known until we get back to the States and can talk it over with Joe.
    Carl and Mac are nearly done. Russ and Tom have further to go but they're coming along too. Looks like I am the only ground gripper in the old gang. With any luck though, I'll be back in the air in a couple of months.
    As you probably know, my wife is living in California now. Her sis went out to get married and Lou went along. She had planned on going to Chicago to live but her sis argued her into going to the coast. She is doing secretarial work in a shipyard.
    The boys all sent their regards and we hope that soon we'll be able to come and keep that date with you.

One of your boys,
Joe Rex

From Carl Moore to Mrs. Nelson

July 23, 1944
England

Dear Mom Nelson,
    I just received another of your swell letters and am glad to hear the pictures arrived ok. I still haven't got the other ones I am having done in town.
    I was pleased to read the clipping you sent. It was good to hear you are receiving so much mail from all of Dick's many friends. I just had another letter from Evelyn Hiley. It's a good thing my own girlfriend is so broadminded as I have been hearing from lots of girls and people I never knew before and sometimes I don't know whether I should correspond with them but I don't think she minds. I'm sure I don't mean anything by it. I just like to help anyone I can, in anyway I can. Most all of them want to know about one or more of the officers.
    Mother always likes to hear from you. I only wish you would of had time to visit my house when you went to Tennessee. How were things down there and how was your trip? Rex said his parents were over to visit you. Joe is with us now. I hope when I get home I can arrange to see you both again. I have two more raids to go and hope in a couple of months I'll be able to go home.
    Our Chaplin Richards is sure a swell fellow. He helped me a lot when I was feeling low. He only lives a few miles from my home. His wife has been going up to see my mother.

Letters

Lt. Borchert's crew #57 finished their missions and I guess the officers are on their way home by now. The enlisted men are here yet. We have been together all through our training and combat.

That's all I can unwind for now. Please write again soon.

Sincerely yours,
Carl

From Mrs. Nelson to Mrs. Mathies

August 10th, 1944
3316 Park Ave
Brookfield, Ill

Dear Mrs. Mathies,

Well, we are home now and your kind letter with enclosed clippings was awaiting us. Thank you so much for same and we Nelsons rejoice with you and yours, upon the happy and proud occasion. I know you were a good soldier and just as brave as Archie would have wanted you to be, when accepting your medal, the highest honor that can come to our boys. Yes, we had a lovely trip and a much needed rest. After leaving you that morning, we sped on East and arrived early Sunday a.m. at our son's in New Jersey. He and his wife were devoted to us and did all in their power to make us happy and comfortable. We were with them just a week as Mr. Nelson had business appointments Tuesday and Wednesday in the South. On our way out of Morristown (where our son lives) we passed thru Burlington, N.J. and as that is where Joe Martin's folks live we stopped and looked them up. They, like yourself, were so surprised and happy to see us. They showed us four postals they had received from Joe, in the prison camp in Germany. He can only write postals, and only one each month. The first postal, he asked "What has become of the crew?" (meaning our boys). So Mrs. Martin wrote him and to camouflage the news, because of censorship, she said, "his cousins Dick, Wally, Bartley and Archie had been killed in an auto accident." As Joe has no cousins by those names, she knew he would catch on and get the message she was trying to convey. But the Martins knew no more what happened than the rest of us and Mr. Martin said "not until Joe is released and comes home will any one know what really happened." So guess we will all have to wait. But should I hear any further news, I'll let you know and you do the same. Take good care of yourself for your family's sake, and you will hear from me.

All loving thoughts to you,
Florence E. Nelson

Valor at Polebrook

From Joe Martin to Joe Rex

July 5th, 1945
Burlington, N.J.

Dear Rex,

Received your telegram last night and was sure glad to hear you're back and around again. I wouldn't let Mother discuss the accident for I heard you were all safe and getting along swell and I wanted to let it go at that. You may not know it Rex but for seven and a half months I looked for some sign of you fellows around the various prison camps I've been in, thinking all the while that I was the last one left with Bart and Nelson and that you had all bailed out when I opened the bomb bay doors. You can't imagine what I thought when I got my first letter (after seven and a half months) from home with hints as to what had happened.

I prayed daily for you fellows and for the souls of the four swellest boys I ever knew. Why it had to happen to us with all the rest of the planes they could have jumped I'll never know, and why it had to happen to Walt instead of me is something I'll never forgive myself for. I knew Bart was dead at the time and thought Nelson was too - but I understand Nelson still had life left - when I was deducting all this I was alone and that is all I remember for I must have passed out for lack of oxygen.

It's been a long haul Rex, thinking about that every night since February 20th. I am trying so hard to forget but I guess it's impossible. I feel pretty bad when someone asks how I was shot down. I wish people would have some consideration, but I guess they just don't think.

Enough of that. Let's get back to you. I read one of your mother's letters to my mother (by the way, I want to thank her sincerely for her swell letters, it made her feel swell) telling how you got hurt on bailing out and that was the first I've heard and that same evening I got your telegram. Look Rex, it sure would be swell seeing you again - so here's the set up. We have a place down at the shore (Seaside Park, N.J.) and I am going down this coming Saturday till August 23, at which time I report to Atlantic City for two weeks and then ? Well, I want you and your wife to come on down for a few days or as long as you can stay. There will be plenty of room, for most of the time it will be just my younger sister and myself there, and always remember there's always room for one more. The address will be on return address. Let me know and maybe something else can be arranged.

Give my best regards to all Rex and thank your mother again for being so kind and considerate to my mother. Wrote a letter to Carl yesterday and I sure would like to have a talk with you, for things just don't jive with things I've read recently.

Sincerely a friend,
Joe

Letters

From Mrs. Nelson to Mrs. Mathies

Tuesday, Feb. 19th, 1946
3316 Park Ave
Brookfield, Ill

My Dear Friend,

I know your thoughts are reverting back to two years tomorrow - Feb. 20th, the same as mine and since I cannot visit with you in person, I want this message of love to comfort you and bring a sweet assurance that "our boys" are together and I know are happy, hence we who are left behind must carry on just the same and be the courageous brave soldiers and fighters for the Peace, which they fought and died for!

Sometimes, I think the passing of our loved ones isn't the hardest blow of all - there are some things even harder than death itself. To come home mentally crippled, in that they do not recognize their own, or so physically maimed that they are helpless, is a constant reminder of this awful war. Our boys did not have to suffer weeks or months of pain and anguish before passing on - as some have had to do - then the suspense of "missing" for a whole year, not knowing where they are or what they are doing, only to be told at the end of a year they were accepted as dead. All these instances should make us feel grateful. We know the details connected with our boys crash, even to the very spot where they lie side by side, asleep. We miss them terribly, yes, but it is only for a short time, then we all will "cross the bar" and join them!

I trust and pray you and your dear family will be reconciled to "His Will". Turn to your Bible and read Second Corinthians Chapter I verses 3 and 4. This will give you strength and peace.

Leaving you in God's Loving Care

Ever Lovingly,
Florence E. Nelson

Archie and his mother, Mrs. Mary Mathies, outside the family home in Finleyville, Pennsylvania.

Valor at Polebrook

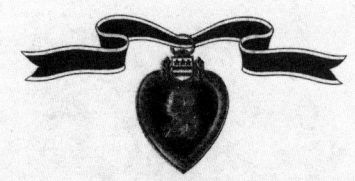

THE UNITED STATES OF AMERICA

TO ALL WHO SHALL SEE THESE PRESENTS, GREETING:
THIS IS TO CERTIFY THAT
THE PRESIDENT OF THE UNITED STATES OF AMERICA
PURSUANT TO AUTHORITY VESTED IN HIM BY CONGRESS
HAS AWARDED THE

PURPLE HEART

ESTABLISHED BY GENERAL GEORGE WASHINGTON
AT NEWBURGH, NEW YORK, AUGUST 7, 1782
TO

Flight Officer Ronald E. Bartley, A.S.No. T-122530,

FOR MILITARY MERIT AND FOR WOUNDS RECEIVED
IN ACTION
resulting in his death February 20, 1944.

GIVEN UNDER MY HAND IN THE CITY OF WASHINGTON
THIS 18th DAY OF April 1944

Flight Officer Ronald E. Bartley

WHO GAVE HIS LIFE IN THE PERFORMANCE OF HIS DUTY

February 20, 1944

HE LIVED TO BEAR HIS COUNTRY'S ARMS. HE DIED TO SAVE ITS HONOR. HE WAS A SOLDIER... AND HE KNEW A SOLDIER'S DUTY. HIS SACRIFICE WILL HELP TO KEEP AGLOW THE FLAMING TORCH THAT LIGHTS OUR LIVES... THAT MILLIONS YET UNBORN MAY KNOW THE PRICELESS JOY OF LIBERTY. AND WE WHO PAY HIM HOMAGE, AND REVERE HIS MEMORY, IN SOLEMN PRIDE REDEDICATE OURSELVES TO A COMPLETE FULFILLMENT OF THE TASK FOR WHICH HE SO GALLANTLY HAS PLACED HIS LIFE UPON THE ALTAR OF MAN'S FREEDOM.

H. H. ARNOLD
General, U. S. Army,
Commanding General Army Air Forces

Postscript

Who would have thought that a book I read in the eighth grade would eventually change my life, my family's lives, and touch the lives of so many other people? When I began to research the story of Ten Horsepower, I had no idea how big a part of my life it would become.

My involvement with this project has seen many dreams come true: To meet the surviving members of the crew of Ten Horsepower. To stand on the main runway of Polebrook airfield where the plane took off for the last time. To walk the face of Denton Hill, where Ten Horsepower crashed, and there reflect on the men who gave their lives for their pilot. And to meet literally hundreds of people whom I now call friends. The story I read as a boy has become a rewarding chapter in my life as a man.

This book would not have been possible if it were not for my dear wife, Fern, who after only eleven months of marriage said "yes" to my desire to research the story, and who (ten years later) is still saying "yes" while I spend our savings for the future on retelling of the past. The sacrifices Fern has made to help my dreams come true are endless. She has been with me all along the way, as we traveled thousands of miles during seven summer family vacations looking for answers. We passed many places of interest where she wanted to stop, but couldn't because our research schedule was so tight, and all the while, Fern just smiled. (Fern didn't smile as much the year she was pregnant. She felt too sick to travel, but even then she kept going. I offered to turn around and go home, but she said no, and was sick for 5,499 miles of our 5,500 mile trip. If that isn't support and encouragement, I don't know what is.) Even now that our children Luke and Rachel are with us, we still travel to attend the annual 351st reunions. Fern, you are truly the best thing that has ever happened for me. This book would not exist if not for you. Thank you.

This book would not be what it is without the work Jeff Rogers put into it. Jeff started out to help me write a magazine article, and along the way found a deep respect and admiration for the crew of Ten Horsepower. Thanks, Jeff, for all the long nights you put into rewriting parts of the story because I had found some new information.

Eric Senf was the missing piece of the puzzle. Without his eagerness to share his knowledge and background in publishing we would still be hoping for the day our book became a reality. Like they say, nothing happens by coincidence. God made our paths cross. He knew what would happen. Thank you, Eric, for all your help.

Yes, just who would have thought that what I read so long ago would change

Valor at Polebrook

my life forever? Jesus Christ knew, for without him in my life showing me the way to go it would not have been possible for me to have touched the lives of all the people I did while researching and publishing this book.

I want to thank God, my Heavenly Father, for sending his son, Jesus Christ, into this world. For those who call on his name and ask Christ into their hearts will have eternal life. Walter and Archie had to make a life or death decision. To bail out would mean certain death for Lt. Nelson. To try to land might be to give their friend a new chance in life.

Just as Walter and Archie would not let their friend die, God will not let us die without giving us another chance at life everlasting. "For God so loved the world that He gave His one and only son, that whoever believes in him shall not perish but have eternal life. For God did not send his son into the world to condemn the world, but to save the world through him." Don't let another day go by without asking Jesus Christ into your life as your personal friend and Lord and savior of your life. You have nothing to lose, but everything to gain. Life here on Earth is short. Don't let this chance pass you by, for the wages of sin is death. Eternity is forever. Thank you Jesus, for dying for my sins and for coming into my life upon my asking and making me a child of God.

Yes, just who would have thought?

Sincerely,
Rick School

Rick and Fern School at the 351st Bomb Group Memorial, Polebrook Airfield, England. Spring, 1992.

Two years into our research, Fern bought this A-2 flight jacket for my birthday. We then found Bill Garmon, the artist who hand-painted the jackets used in the movie *Memphis Belle*. Bill painted my jacket to commemorate the crew of Ten Horsepower. Fern says that getting my jacket painted is my Christmas present until the year 2020.

Postscript

Jeff Rogers' first publication success was an article about his experiences while learning to fly in 1984. That story was followed by aviation technical articles and magazine versions of the Ten Horsepower story. Valor at Polebrook is Jeff's first book.

When not writing, Jeff enjoys flying and photography, installing electrical systems in historic and homebuilt aircraft, and going on adventures with his daughters Monique and Lindsey.

 # Bibliography

America's Medal of Honor Recipients,
Highland Publishers, Golden Valley, MN 1980

Birdsall, Steve: B-17 Flying Fortress in Color
Squadron/Signal publications, 1986

Borts, Lawrence H. Foster, Col. (Ret.) Frank C.
Medals of America: U.S. Military Medals 1939 to Present
Medals of America Press, Fountain Inn, SC 1995

Davis, Larry: B-17 in Action
Squadron/Signal publications, 1984

Freeman, Roger: Airfields of the Eighth - Then and Now
Battle of Britain Prints International, Ltd. 1978

Freeman, Roger: The Mighty Eighth
Jane's Publishing Company, Ltd. 1970

Harris, Peter and Harbour, Ken: The 351st Bomb Group in W.W.II
Byron Kennedy and Company, 1980

Jablonski, Edward: Flying Fortress
Doubleday and Company, Inc. 1965

Matlock, Edward: The Red Devils, a personal, unpublished diary written during 1943 and 1944.

McDowell, Ernest R.: Flying Fortress: The Boeing B-17
Squadron/Signal publications, 1987

Nelson, Florence: A Resume Of Our Pilot's Life In The Service Of His Country, a personal, unpublished journal written in 1944.

Pilot's Flight Operating Instruction Manual For Army Models B-17F and G,
U.S. Army, 1943

Rust, Ken C.: Eighth Air Force Story
Sunshine House, 1978

Newspapers and Magazines:

The Aurora Daily Beacon, July 5, 1944, Aurora, Illinois
The Beacon News, February 20, 1994, Aurora, Illinois
The Columbus Dispatch, February 21, 1944, Columbus, Ohio
The News Chronicle, February 21, 1944, (English newspaper)
Newsweek Magazine, July 14, 1944
The Seattle Daily Times, February 21, 1944, Seattle, Wash.
The Suburban Magnet, March 16, 1944, Brookfield, Illinois
The Underwood News, March 30, 1944, Underwood, N. Dakota